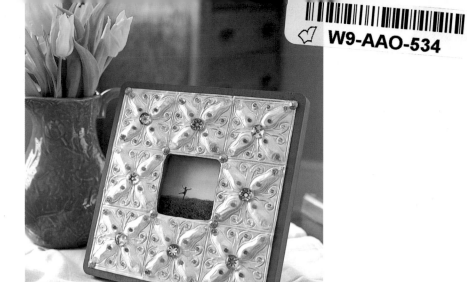

the BEADED home

Simply

Beautiful

Projects

Katherine Duncan Aimone

LARK BOOKS

A Division of Sterling Publishing Company, Inc.

NEW YORK

ART DIRECTOR:
Susan McBride

PHOTOGRAPHY:
Keith Wright

PHOTO STYLIST:
Wendy Wright

ILLUSTRATIONS:
Orrin Lundgren

EDITORIAL
ASSISTANCE:
Rain Newcomb

*Many thanks to
Rain Newcomb,
expert beader, who assisted
me with great patience
through all stages
of the book.*

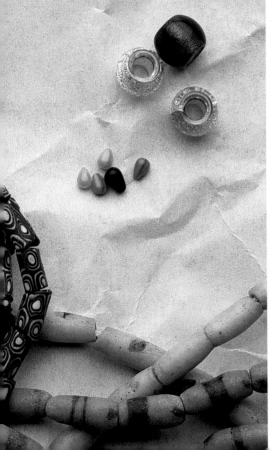

Library of Congress Cataloging-in-Publication Data

Duncan-Aimone, Katherine.
    The beaded home : simply beautiful projects / by Katherine Duncan Aimone.
      p. cm.
    ISBN 1-57990-381-9 (pbk.)
    1. Beadwork. 2. Interior decoration. I. Title.

TT860 .D84 2001
745.58'2–dc21

                                                        2001029633

10 9 8 7 6 5 4

Published by Lark Books, a division of Sterling Publishing Co., Inc.
387 Park Avenue South, New York, N.Y. 10016

Distributed in Canada by Sterling Publishing,
c/o Canadian Manda Group, One Atlantic Ave.,
Suite 105Toronto, Ontario, Canada M6K 3E7

Distributed in the U.K. by:
Guild of Master Craftsman Publications Ltd.
Castle Place, 166 High StreetLewes,
East SussexEngland BN7 1XU
Tel: (+ 44) 1273 477374
Fax: (+ 44) 1273 478606
Email: pubs@thegmcgroup.com
Web: www.gmcpublications.com

Distributed in Australia by Capricorn Link (Australia) Pty Ltd., P.O. Box 704, Windsor, NSW 2756
Australia

If you have questions or comments about this book, please contact:
Lark Books
67 Broadway
Asheville, NC 28801
(828) 236-9730

Printed in China

ISBN 1-57990-381-9 (pbk.)

the BEADED home

CONTENTS

INTRODUCTION

For centuries people have treasured beads and used them for purposes that range from economic to religious. Ancient peoples believed beads were imbued with mystical powers, fifteenth-century Europeans traded glass beads in America, and nineteenth-century Victorians used beads to adorn everything from bags to bedspreads.

Today, we value beads for many of the same reasons. We still relish holding beads in the palms of our hands while they glimmer like newly discovered treasures, still long to touch them in order to experience their matte or glassy surfaces, and still love to use them to adorn the surfaces of our clothing and objects.

Some among us are obsessed with them, and haunt the recesses of every bead store that we can find. We may have a reason for purchasing our latest beads, but, many times, they'll end up in a box or in small jars on a windowsill where they catch the light. Either way—with intended purpose or without—they end up in our kitchens, bedrooms, living rooms, and bathrooms.

This book of 47 projects explores the idea of taking your beads out of their boxes to use them in new and novel ways. The four sections of the book key into the human desires that have traditionally led to our use of beads in dwellings—to decorate, illuminate, celebrate, and inspire.

Traditional techniques such as bead embroidery and making fringe are applied to contemporary window decorations, tablecloths, lampshades, pillows, and flowerpots. The popular trend of wrapping wire and beads is explored through a variety of ideas that range from crystal-laden serving utensils to embellished picture frames. Tiny glass seed beads, bugle beads, bone beads, and semi-precious stones adorn the surfaces of clocks, boxes, bottles, and drawers.

The use of beads for decorating your home can be as wide as your imagination. This book will give you the basic information that you need to get started (even if you've never been a beader before), and lead you step by-step through making any project you choose. Whether the project takes a few hours or requires several sittings, time will fly once you discover how simple and satisfying it is to fill your home with the glitter and glamour of beads.

Cut beads

Cubes (4 mm)

Triangle beads
(size 5)

Bugle beads

Horn beads

Swarovski crystals

Variagated
seed beads
(size 11)

Japanese
color-lined
seed beads
(size 11)

Matte seed
beads
(size 8)

Matte
seed
beads
(size 6)

GETTING STARTED

Beading projects can be simple or complex. You can make beautiful things with easy techniques, such as wrapping wire and gluing beads, or you can take on more complicated fringes and embroidery. Either way, this first section will quell your fears about the vocabulary and tools needed to bring you up to speed. Once you get your mind around a few of the basics, all you'll need is some time and patience to conquer any of the projects in this book.

Color-lined
seed beads
(size 11)

Delicas

Hand-blown
glass bead

Lampwork
beads

Bone beads

Leaf and flower beads

Branched coral

Star beads

Vintage spears

African trade beads

Handmade copper and enamel beads

Cane glass

Fire-polished beads

Hand-blown glass beads

Ball silver spacers

Beads come in a variety of sizes and are made from different materials including glass, metal, and semi-precious stones.

Jasper rondels

Faceted beads

Polymer beads

Beads of malachite, lapis, and snowflake obsidian

Bicones

Gold lined faceted beads

Cloisonné

Pony and crow beads

Roller balls

Copper tubes

African trade beads

Teardrops

Sizing Things Up

If you've ever visited a bead store, you may have gone through a series of mental states that range from elation to confusion. So many choices, so many bins, so many colors—where do you begin?

But don't despair; beads can be broken down into basic categories that will save you from being overwhelmed. And, as you select beaded projects to make from this book, you'll have a list of beads at your command.

If you don't understand something, don't hesitate to ask a salesperson for their assistance—many of them are avid beaders, and they love to talk about their subject matter! They can also help you find appropriate substitutions for beads if you want to change the look of a project.

Several of the projects in this book use small glass beads called seed beads that come in an array of colors and finishes. Keep in mind a couple of caveats about the finishes on seed beads. First, the finish on most metallic seed beads will wear off if the bead is handled often, so don't choose them for projects that will be repeatedly touched. Second, color-lined seed beads are transparent beads with a lining on the inside that can wash out if the bead gets soaked in water often.

Seed beads have a unique sizing system—each size is labeled by number, and the larger the number, the smaller the bead. (Size 11 seed beads are the most commonly used ones.) Others are measured in millimeters, with the size referring to the diameter of the bead (figure 1). Even though bugle beads are categorized as seed beads, these long, skinny tubes are measured in millimeters too. They are available in most of the same colors and finishes of regular seed beads.

So, although you may think of beads as round by definition, they come in lots of other shapes that range from cubes to elongated barrels (figure 2). The general rule of thumb seems to be that if you can put a hole through the middle of it and string it, you can call it a bead! You'll also discover that beads are made out of a wide range of materials—glass, bone, horn, wood, stone, and metal.

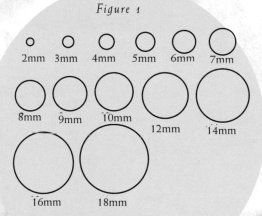

Figure 1

2mm 3mm 4mm 5mm 6mm 7mm

8mm 9mm 10mm 12mm 14mm

16mm 18mm

Most beads are measured in millimeters, with the size referring to the diameter of the bead.

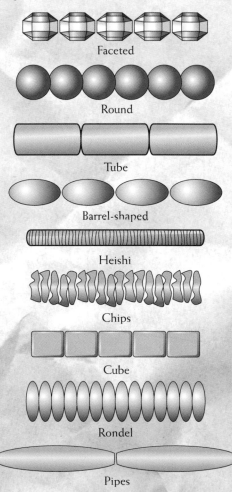

Figure 2

Faceted

Round

Tube

Barrel-shaped

Heishi

Chips

Cube

Rondel

Pipes

Beads come in lots of shapes that range from cubes to elongated barrels.

Beading Materials, Tools & Techniques

The following section will introduce many of the materials and tools that you'll need to complete the projects in this book. A few common beading techniques are introduced as well. As you read through the project section, you'll find more detailed information about materials, tools, and techniques as they apply to individual projects.

Scissors

Braided monofilament

Beading thread

Synthetic thread conditioner

An assortment of beading needles (left to right): Size 10 beading needle, size 12 appliqué needle, size 12 beading needle, size 13 beading needle, twisted wire needles

Beeswax and beading thread

Crimping pliers

Round-nose pliers

Flat-nose pliers

Needle-nose pliers

Wire cutters

Nylon-coated beading wire and crimp beads

Wire

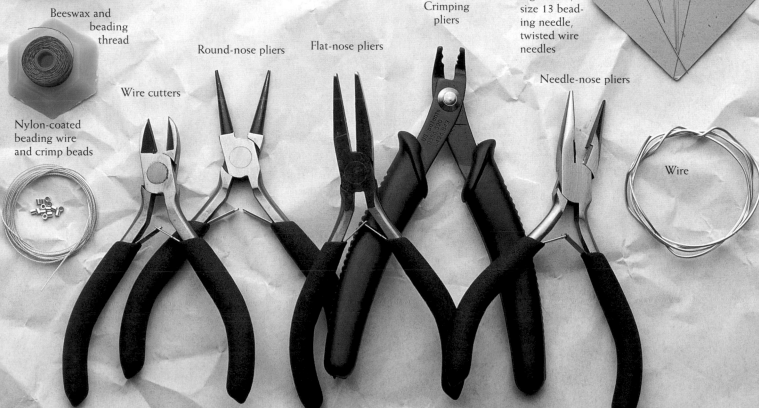

Nylon Beading Thread

When you embroider or do other work with seed beads, you'll use nylon beading thread sold on cards or spools. The most common form is a single nylon strand, originally developed for use on tapestries. The second type is a double-nylon strand, twisted together and waxed. Choosing which type to use depends entirely on personal preference, but the single strand is much easier to thread through the needle. Both are strong and long-lasting threads.

The different diameters of beading thread are labeled by letter, but the labeling system is not the same for single and double strands. For the single strand thread, size D is the most common and versatile weight. Size B is thinner than size D, and A (or O) is the thinnest type. Size A is the most commonly used and versatile weight for double/twisted thread.

Waxing or conditioning the thread helps to prevent it from fraying, splitting, and tangling while you work with it. To condition it, cut a length from your spool, and drag it across a block of beeswax or synthetic thread conditioner.

Beading thread comes in a range of colors. Pick one that matches or contrasts with the beads you have. Colors that match or are a shade lighter than the beads tend

Use nylon beading thread to embroider with seed beads.

to blend into the background of your project. Contrasting colors add visual interest and depth to your project.

Monofilament & Beading Cord

Nylon monofilament, commonly known as fishing line, is often used to string beads. Unfortunately, fishing line has a limited life span and decays after a year. Unless you relish the thought of picking up beads off

the floor and redoing your project once a year, don't use fishing line!

The alternative to this scenario is braided monofilament, which you can find in most bead stores. It wears well, is easy to knot, lasts a long time, and is available in several different thicknesses.

Most stores also carry a braided or twisted nylon cord that comes in a variety of thicknesses and colors and is great for knotting. It works especially well with large beads that have small holes.

Flexible Beading Wires

Flexible beading wires come in many forms. Tigertail—a tiny steel cable coated with nylon—is strong and flexible as well as durable. It's stiff enough to string beads without a needle, but won't knot well. Instead of knotting the ends of it, you can easily finish the ends with crimp beads (see page 14). Since tigertail tends to get kinks in it, it's better used with larger, heavier beads that drape well.

Flexible synthetic beading wire is another option. This incredibly-strong stringing material is sold under a variety of brand names that come in various colors and thicknesses. The smaller the diameter, the easier this wire is to knot.

Wire & Beads

Wire and beads are a natural combination. Wire can be used to attach beads to objects while contributing to the overall design of your piece. There are a number of projects in this book that show off twisting, wrapping, and looping wire between beads to create beautiful effects.

Wire is available in bead stores and craft shops, and comes in a variety of metals and thicknesses. It is usually sold in spools and identified by gauge. The higher the number of the wire's gauge, the thinner it is.

Wire can be used to attach beads to objects, while contributing to the overall design of your piece.

Needles

For any project that uses beading thread, you'll need a needle. When working with seed beads, use a beading needle or an appliqué needle. Beading needles are numbered according to their size, and size 12 is the most commonly used. The higher the number of the needle, the smaller it is.

For most of the projects in this book that require needles, you'll use a size 12 beading needle. If you find that you're having trouble getting the beads that you choose over the needle, switch to a size 13 or higher. To embroider with beads, a size 12 appliqué needle works well with size 11 beads and larger. These needles are stiff enough to pierce the fabric easily.

The eyes on the beading and appliqué needles are tiny. It takes a bit of practice and a lot of patience to be able to thread them quickly. If you're having trouble, take a deep breath, cut the thread at an angle, coat the end in beeswax, and squeeze it flat before trying again.

When you're working with larger beads, you can use a needle that is easier to thread. Big-eyed needles are perhaps the greatest invention on earth for the sore-eyed beader. Threading the large eye is painless because this long, thick needle has a center that opens up and closes to take the thread. When working with one of these needles, keep a close eye on your thread. The edge of the needle's eye can cut through thread if pulled too harshly.

In a similar realm is the twisted-wire needle. It closes up when forced through the first bead, but can be easily reopened with an awl or a pin when you need to rethread.

Knots & Finishes

Once all the beads are on the thread, what's the best way to keep them there? The answer to that question depends on what kind of project you're doing.

For embroidery projects, you'll use the same knot that you use for regular embroidery or sewing. Begin by threading your needle, and tying a knot at the end. Pull it

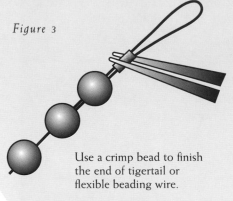

Figure 3

Use a crimp bead to finish the end of tigertail or flexible beading wire.

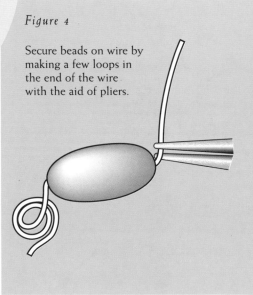

Figure 4

Secure beads on wire by making a few loops in the end of the wire with the aid of pliers.

through the fabric so that the knot is hidden on the wrong side of the fabric. To anchor the thread, take a small stitch in the fabric where the thread comes out on the front. When you reach the end of your thread, anchor the thread with a small stitch at that point, and tie off the thread at the back.

To keep the knot from unraveling, you can use glue or nail polish. A small tube of fast-drying bead glue or bead cement sold in craft stores will do the trick. Apply the glue or cement to a needle, straight pin, or toothpick before you coat your knot. Clear nail polish with nylon also works well for securing knots. (Avoid using regular craft glue, it will coat the surface of the knot but won't hold it tight.) Strong adhesive or epoxy, available in large tubes in most bead stores, will fill any other need you might have, such as gluing flat beads on a frame or affixing wire to wood.

If you're doing a project in which a conventional knot will detract from your design, you can use a hidden knot. On some projects, you may need to hide the knot inside the beads. To do this, thread your nee-

dle and begin stringing beads, leaving a thread tail of about 5 inches (12.7 cm). When you are ready to knot, thread the tail onto another needle before pushing it through the surrounding beads. Exit between two adjacent beads, and loop the loose thread around the bead-supporting thread. Insert the end of your needle through the loop twice to tie a knot. Pull the thread tight, and sew through the next bead. The knot should pull through and be hidden by the beads. Finish both ends of the thread this way.

You can keep beads on tigertail and flexible beading wire by using a crimp bead—a small metal sleeve with a hole through it that holds

tightly once it has been pinched. To use a crimp bead, simply place it on the end of your strand, add a small bead, then push the wire back through it. Slide the crimp bead against the last bead you added. Make sure there aren't any gaping holes between beads, and pinch the crimp bead closed with pliers (figure 3).

When working with wire, you can secure the bead or beads by making a few loops in the wire with the aid of the pliers to keep the beads from sliding off (figure 4).

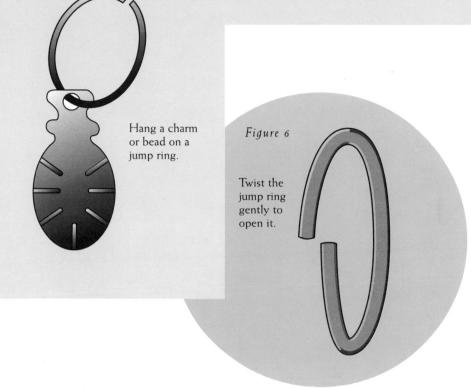

Figure 5

Hang a charm or bead on a jump ring.

Figure 6

Twist the jump ring gently to open it.

Pliers & Cutters

To work with wire, you'll need a couple of different types of pliers that can be purchased at a bead or craft store. Round-nose pliers (also called jewelry pliers) have a non-serrated jaw, so they work well for making loops in wire without marring the surface. Needle-nose pliers (rounded on the outside surfaces but flat on the inside) are good for gripping wire. Wire cutters allow you to trim and snip the wire. Make sure to get a pair that cuts flush.

Flat-nose pliers have a wider jaw and work well for gripping and working with larger-gauge wire. If you find you can't manipulate the bulk of your wire with your round- or needle-nose pliers, you may need a pair of flat-nose pliers. Crimping pliers are used specifically for crimping and are used by professional jewelrymakers. For the occasional crimp, round- or needle-nose pliers will suffice.

Jump Rings

Here's a scenario to consider: You find the perfect charm or bead for your project, you dash home to start, and that's when you see it. The hole runs the wrong way, and if you put it on your project it'll hang funny or not work at all. Don't despair. The jump ring—a tiny wire circle with a split in it—saves the day. Place a jump ring through the hole in a charm or bead, and you'll be able to hang the charm straight (figure 5).

To open a jump ring, use two pairs of pliers to grasp the ring on either side of the split, and twist gently in opposite directions (figure 6). Add the charm, loop the jump ring onto your chosen spot, and close the ring by twisting the ends of the circle back together. Never open a jump ring by pulling the ends farther apart, or enlarging the circle. If you do this, you'll weaken the metal, making it more likely to break. And it's next to impossible to neatly close a jump ring after you've opened it the wrong way.

Making Fringe

Shimmering dangles of hanging beads—what's not to love about that idea? In this book, beaded fringes are used to decorate pillows, lampshades, and curtains. Fringes are easy to make with a little practice.

A fringe is composed of a series of strands of beads that create a decorative border. Gravity is overcome on each strand by the placement of at least one "stopper" bead on the end of each strand. To begin a fringe, pull your needle and thread out of the edge of the fabric or other material, add a series of beads to make up the first strand, and add the stopper bead as the last bead. Next, you'll take the needle back through all of the beads except the stopper, and exit out of the top of the line of beads (figure 6). For a variation on this idea, form a circle of beads to serve as a stopper by skipping several beads before running the thread back through the original beads (figure 7).

As you can probaby imagine, variations on fringe are as endless as the number of combinations of beads that you can dream up.

A beaded fringe turns an ordinary valance into a conversation piece.

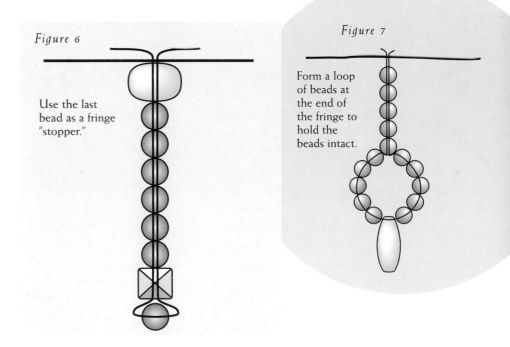

Figure 6

Use the last bead as a fringe "stopper."

Figure 7

Form a loop of beads at the end of the fringe to hold the beads intact.

Bead Embroidery

There are as many variations of bead embroidery as there are embroidery stitches. The simplest form of bead embroidery (used in several projects in this book) involves using a running stitch to hold a line of beads on fabric (figure 8). In this case, the thread doesn't show, and the beads form a strand on the fabric's surface.

Beads can also be used to embellish common embroidery stitches, such as the button stitch. Once the line of stitching is completed with embroidery thread, use beading thread to sew small individual beads onto particular parts of the stitch. On page 117 you'll find a stitch chart which references the embroidery stitches used in the projects found in this book. Essentially, you can add beads to any stitch that you desire.

Work Space

There are a few things that will make your time beading more productive and fun. The first and most important of those is light. Even larger beads are relatively small, so be kind to your eyes. The best kind of light to use is a full spectrum light, but any soft white light will work.

To make your beads easier to find, sort them into small shallow dishes or on pieces of cloth. And always keep your scissors sharp. Cutting with a dull pair of scissors will fray the ends of your thread, making it even more difficult to get through that tiny eye of the needle.

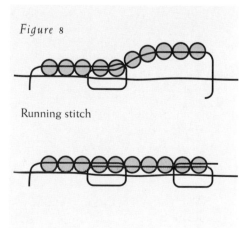

Figure 8

Running stitch

decorate

THE PROJECTS

celebrate

illuminate

From a beaded lampshade to jeweled cutlery, you'll find something to fit every mood and room of your home on the following pages. The projects range from very simple to intricate, but all can be done with some patience if you follow the directions and illustrations provided.

So catch some inspiration from the talented creations of our designers, clear off your dining room table, and surprise yourself with the satisfaction of creating with beads. Make each project your own by choosing colors that accent a favorite spot in your home.

inspire

decorate

Beautify
your home both
inside and out
with beaded
creations
such as an
embellished
gourd for your
living room or
an intricate
dragonfly
windchime for
your porch.

strung bead
DRAWER PULLS

Designer: TERRY TAYLOR

materials & tools

For each drawer handle:

2 screw eyes of a length
to fit the depth of your drawer

2 washers and nuts to fit
screw eyes

2 crimp beads

Tigertail (flexible beading wire)

Needle-nose pliers

Variety of medium-sized
beads of your choice

Strands of handsome beads function as drawer pulls to complement an antique piece of furniture.

instructions

1. Remove the original handles and hardware from the drawer.

2. Insert a screw eye into one of the empty holes in the drawer. Place a washer inside the drawer on the screw eye, and secure it with the nut.

3. String one crimp bead onto the beading wire, loop the end of the wire through one of the screw eyes, and feed the beading wire back through the crimp bead. Pull tight and crimp with the flat-nose pliers.

4. String your beads onto the wire, making sure that your drawer pull is long enough to hang in a loop between the screw eyes.

5. Add another crimp bead, go through the second screw eye and back through the crimp. Compress the crimp bead.

6. Repeat for all of the drawers.

wild thing FRAME

Metal, bone, and glass beads combined with copper wire create a complex, meandering trail on this frame.

materials & tools

Wire cutters

22-gauge commercial copper wire, 14-foot-long (4.2 m) piece

Wooden frame with at least a 2-inch (5.1 cm) width (Ours is covered in braided rope, but you can also use a regular frame.)

Electric drill and drill bit

50–75 assorted metal, bone, and lampwork beads (10 to 16 mm)

Needle-nose pliers

Round-nose pliers

instructions

1. Use the wire cutters to cut the wire into eight 20-inch-long (50.8 cm) lengths.

2. On the front of the frame, drill 10 to 12 holes that are centered along the frame and spaced 3 inches (7.6 cm) apart. (Choose a drill bit that is slightly larger than the circumference of your wire.)

3. Push a piece of the wire through a corner hole to begin. Pull both ends of the wire to the front of the frame. Push another piece of wire through the next hole, and pull both ends of the wire to the front of the frame.

Designer: SUSAN RIND

4. Feed several beads onto the wires. Use pliers to randomly loop and twist the adjacent wires, and lock them together by passing one underneath the other at points where they meet. (Doing this will help hold the wire in place.)

5. Keep adding wires and beads in this fashion, locking the adjacent wires together as you go. Tuck the ends of the wires underneath the beads to hide them.

6. Add all the wires to the frame until you've embellished all sides.

dressy BEADED THUMBTACKS

How simple could it be to create

something that makes everyday life

more special?

Designer: LYNN B. KRUCKE

materials & tools

Two-part epoxy glue

Flat-headed thumbtacks

Toothpicks

Assorted wood, bone, glass, and clay beads (choose beads that have at least one flat side for mounting)

Sand or rice poured into shallow baking pan

instructions

1. Mix up a small portion of the epoxy glue according to package directions.

2. Apply a small amount to the top of each thumbtack with a toothpick, then adhere the flat side of a bead. (A strong glue is important to use, since the tacks will be consistently pushed and pulled.)

3. Gently place the beaded tacks faceup in a shallow pan filled with a layer of sand or rice for drying. This extra step will prevent the beads from sliding off the tacks.

mock abacus WALL PIECE

Designer: NANCY WORRELL

materials & tools

4 artist's stretcher bars: two 12 inches (30.5 cm) long and two 10 inches (25.4 cm) long

Pencil

Small handheld drill

Acrylic paint in color of your choice for frame

Paintbrush

Acrylic matte varnish

Picture hanger

7 dowels, each 9 inches (22.9 cm) long, ⅛ inch (3 mm) diameter

80 pony beads in various colors (9 x 6 mm)

3 different kinds of animal beads, 6 of each (18 to 25 mm)

Measuring tape

This playful way to display colorful animal beads will enliven the wall of your child's nursery.

instructions

1. Measure 2¾ inches (7 cm) down from the top of the inside edge of one of the 10-inch (25.4 cm) stretcher bars, and make seven sequential marks that are each ¾ inch (1.9 cm) apart. Repeat on the inside edge of the other 10-inch (25.4 cm) stretcher.

2. Using the marks as a guide, drill holes at each point (in the center of the inside ledge of one of the stretchers) that are approximately ⅛ to ¼ inch (3 to 6 mm) deep and slightly over ⅛ inch (3 mm) in diameter. Repeat this process on the other marked stretcher, making sure that the holes are exactly opposite one another to ensure that your dowels will be straight.

3. Assemble the stretcher bars to form a frame. Paint the frame and the dowels with a coat of acrylic paint. After the frame is completely dry, seal it with a coat of acrylic matte varnish.

4. Center and attach the picture hanger to the back of the frame.

5. Beginning at the top of the frame, insert one end of the dowel into one of the top holes, and thread 20 pony beads onto the dowel. Gently bend and insert the dowel into the corresponding hole on the opposite side of the frame.

6. Repeat step 5, threading six animal beads on the next dowel down. Alternate rows of pony beads with rows of animal beads on each of the subsequent dowels.

embroidered
TABLE RUNNER

Designer: DEBI SCHMITZ

Glistening seed beads adorn a flowered fabric in this simple-to-sew table runner.

materials & tools

Fabric scissors

1 yard (.9 m) of floral fabric with a wider weave that frays easily (linen works well)

Size 12 beading needle or appliqué needle

Nylon beading thread to coordinate with beads and fabric

Seed beads to match the colors of the fabric (size 11)

Cutting mat

Rotary cutter

2 yards (1.8 m) of solid linen fabric

Straight pins

Sewing machine and thread

instructions

1. Cut out ten 6-inch (15.2 cm) squares of the floral fabric, optimizing the pattern for each square.

2. Use a running stitch (figure 1) to add lines of colored beads to areas of the floral squares that accentuate the designs. Fray the edges of the squares about ¼ inch (6 mm).

3. On top of the cutting mat, cut out two pieces of 18 x 48-inch (45.7 x 121.9 cm) solid fabric with the rotary cutter.

4. Pin the floral motifs onto the solid fabric.

5. Using thread that matches the floral fabric, sew the squares in place with a ¼-inch (6 mm) allowance from the frayed edge.

6. With wrong sides together, pin together the two pieces of fabric (the front and back of the runner). Sew a ½-inch (1.3 cm) seam allowance around the edge. Stitch another line ¾ inch (1.9 cm) from the outside edge or ¼ inch (6 mm) from the last stitch line.

7. Fray the outside edges of the runner to ½ inch (1.3 cm) or the first stitch line.

8. Stitch small clusters of beads on the solid fabric around the motifs on the runner, as shown in the finished piece.

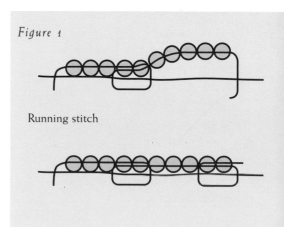

Figure 1

Running stitch

wildflower VALANCE

Designer: SANDIE ABEL

Brighten a window or door with this fringed valance

that sparkles with glass flowers and leaves.

materials & tools

Gold metallic rickrack that measures the length of the valance plus 1 inch (2.5 cm)

Sewing machine threaded with gold thread

Window valance in fabric of your choice

Size 12 beading needle or appliqué needle

Tan nylon beading thread

2 different colors of seed beads (size 11)

Leaf beads in various shapes and colors

Variety of flower beads with holes that run horizontally through their bases

Scissors

instructions

1. Turn the rickrack under ½ inch (1.3 cm) at each end, and use the sewing machine to catch the ends with a few stitches to prevent fraying. Sew the rickrack onto the lower edge of the valance, so that the bottom edge hangs below the valance.

2. Thread your beading needle with beading thread, and tie a knot at the end. Starting at one end of the rickrack, push your needle through the back of the lower edge of the first scallop, and pull the thread through the front.

3. String on a few seed beads, followed by a leaf bead and a few more seed beads. String on a flower bead and a few more seed beads. Continue alternating seed and leaf or flower beads until you have at least 1 inch (2.5 cm) of beads strung.

4. To create the dangle at the end of the fringe, add four seed beads, one teardrop, and three more seed beads. Push the needle back up through the first of the four seed beads you put on in this step, and back through all of the beads you've strung to the top. Pull the thread up to create a loop of seed beads around the teardrop. Push the needle through to the back of the rickrack.

5. Take a tiny stitch, and bring your needle back to the front of the rickrack. String on a seed bead and stitch back through the cloth. Continue adding seed beads at even intervals along the bottom edge of the rickrack until you reach the middle of the next scallop.

6. Create another strand of beads to make a fringe (following steps 3 and 4) before sewing seed beads along the next curved edge of the rickrack. Continue adding fringe (varying the placement of the beads and the lengths of the strands) along the edges until you reach the other end of the rickrack. (Tie off the thread on the back as needed.)

FLOWERPOT *fringe*

Designer: SANDIE ABEL

materials & tools

Small flowerpot

Measuring tape

Braided trim, ¾ inch (1.9 cm) wide

Fast-drying bead glue

Sewing needle and thread that matches trim

Size 12 beading needle and nylon beading thread that complements beads

Flower beads with hole running through center (not end)

Matte yellow seed beads (size 11)

Clear light green seed beads (size 11)

Leaf beads with stringing hole in end

Adhesive-backed hook-and-loop tape, ¾ inch (1.9 cm) wide

Complement an indoor potted plant with a removable necklace full of cheerful flowers and dangling leaves.

instructions

1. Measure the circumference of the top of the flowerpot with the measuring tape, and cut off a piece of braided trim of this length. Apply glue to the cut ends of the braided trim to prevent fraying. When the glue is dry, turn each end under ½ inch (1.3 cm), and sew it down with the sewing needle and thread.

2. Thread the beading needle with the beading thread. Tic a knot in the end of the thread. Push your needle through the back of the trim at one end, and pull the thread out.

3. String on a flower bead and one yellow seed bead. Go back through the center of the flower with your needle. Pull tight so that the seed bead snuggles into the center of the flower, holding it in place.

4. Stitch back through the ribbon, bringing the thread out where you want to place the second flower bead. Sew it down as you did in step 3. Continue to add seed and flower beads up and down along the length of the ribbon until you are satisfied with the way the strip looks.

5. To add the leaves beside the flowers in the braid's center, push your needle through the braid where you want to place the leaf bead. String on four light green seed beads and a leaf bead before pushing the needle back through the braid. Pull the thread tight.

6. Position your needle on the back of the braid where you want to place another leaf next to a flower, and pull the thread back through. Continue to add leaves in this fashion along the length of the ribbon.

7. To add leaf dangles across the bottom of the braid, knot your thread and pull it through the back to the front of the braid. Thread on several light green seed beads, add a leaf, and then thread on the same number of seed beads before pushing the needle back through the braid close to the exiting thread (figure 1). To add a longer dangle, thread on 8 to 10 seed beads, and add a leaf bead. Add half of the number of seed beads that you've already strung, and then run the thread back through the first half of the beads you strung to create a loop (figure 2). Add dangles of various lengths down the length of the braid.

8. Cut off a piece of adhesive-backed hook-and-loop tape the same length as the braid. Apply the loop segment of the hook-and-loop tape to the back of the braid by peeling the backing off carefully before applying it.

9. Apply the other segment of the tape to the top edge of the flower-pot, position the braid on top, and adhere the beaded fringe.

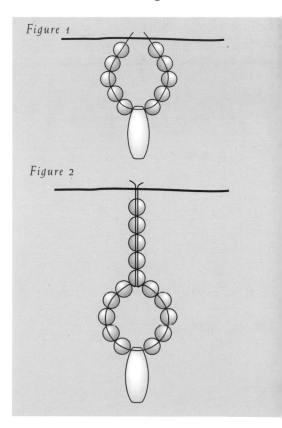

Figure 1

Figure 2

beaded STEPPING STONE

Designer: CHARLI TRAYLOR

materials & tools

10–15 pounds (4.5 to 6.8 kg) sand mix cement

1 pint–1 quart (.47 to .95 L) of water

Large bucket

Wooden paint stirrer or wooden stick

8-inch (20.3 cm) square aluminum baking pan

Spatula

Paper towels

Assorted beads and cabochons*

instructions

1. Read the directions and warning labels on the sand mix cement before beginning this project.

2. Pour sand mix cement and water into a large bucket, and stir it until it is well mixed. Add more cement as needed until it has a thick consistency.

3. Pour the mixture into the baking pan, and smooth it out with a spatula.

4. Allow it to set for one hour. Use paper towels to blot excess water from the surface of the mixture.

5. To create a design, press beads and cabochons into the cement just above the surface.

6. Allow the cement to dry for 48 hours before removing the stone from the pan.

*The dragonfly pattern that you see in this project is made of the following: 6 round beads (6 mm), 2 blue dagger beads, 2½-inch-long (6.4 cm) white beads, 24 small purple teardrops, 8 leaf beads, and 12 glass butterfly beads.

orbiting
GOURD

Plug colorful beads into holes drilled in a woodburned gourd, add loops of reed, and watch your vessel come to life with eye-catching movement.

Designer: DYAN PETERSON

materials & tools

Cured gourd (available at farmers' markets or craft stores)

Scouring pad, stainless steel or copper

Pencil

Sharp knife

Dust mask

Small motorized cutting tool or small handheld power jigsaw

Grapefruit spoon

Coarse sandpaper

Fine-grit sandpaper

Black water-based spray enamel

Rubber gloves

Foam applicator brush

Light brown leather dye

Woodburning tool with large, rounded point

Small paintbrush

Black leather dye

Paper towels

Clear satin-finish spray lacquer

#3 round reed (used for basketmaking)

Cylindrical beads (with holes of a size that fit snuggly on the reed)

Electric drill with bits

Round file

Quick-set epoxy glue

Measuring tape

Craft knife

instructions

1. Remove the dirt and mold from the surface of the gourd with warm water and a scouring pad. Be careful not to scratch the skin of the gourd. Allow the gourd to dry.

2. Use the pencil to draw a line around the top of the gourd to indicate where you want the rim of the vessel to be. Make a slit along this line with the sharp knife.

3. Put on the dust mask. Insert the saw into the slit, and cut slowly until you have reached the inside of the gourd. Continue to cut around the rim.

4. When you have cut along the length of the gourd, remove the top. Scrape all of the pulp and seeds out with the grapefruit spoon.

5. Once the gourd is clean, use the coarse sandpaper to smooth the inside walls. Sand again with the fine-grit sandpaper for a smooth, luscious interior.

6. Spray the inside of the gourd with the water-based enamel. Allow to dry.

7. After the gourd is completely dry, put on the pair of rubber gloves to protect your hands. Use

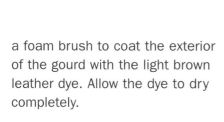

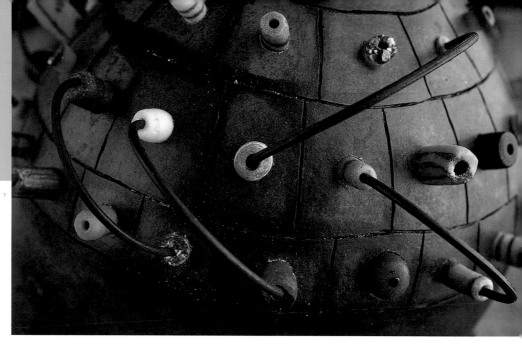

a foam brush to coat the exterior of the gourd with the light brown leather dye. Allow the dye to dry completely.

8. Draw a circle about 1 inch (2.5 cm) down from the rim of the gourd, followed by a circle about ¾ inch (1.9 cm) further down the gourd. Draw another circle about ½ inch (1.3 cm) from this circle so that the area between these two circles forms a band at the top (see the finished photograph).

9. Draw subsequent circles 1½ to 2 inches (3.8 to 5.1 cm) apart that circle the circumference of the gourd, until you reach the lower middle portion of it.

10. Draw staggered vertical lines connecting the circles to create irregularly shaped boxes.

11. Read the manufacturer's instructions on the woodburning tool. Insert the large, rounded point into the tool. Plug in the woodburner, and allow it to heat up.

12. Burn the lines that you drew on the gourd with the woodburning tip. Move the point at a slow but smooth pace. (As you burn the gourd, you may find that debris from the skin builds up on the surface

of the tip. You can remove this debris by running the tip over coarse sandpaper.)

13. Use the small paintbrush and black leather dye to darken the band at the top and outline the boxes. Wipe any excess dye off of the brush using paper towels. Allow the dye to dry thoroughly.

14. To seal the gourd and protect your work, apply a fine mist of clear satin-finish spray lacquer, and allow it to dry. Apply two or three more coats, drying the gourd thoroughly between each coat. (Be careful not to use too much lacquer in any one coat, or it will run and create drips.)

15. Check to make sure that your cylindrical beads fit snugly onto the #3 round reed. Select a drill bit that is slightly smaller than the outside diameter of the bead, and drill a hole in the center of each box.

16. Using the round file, open the hole just enough for the bead to fit in.

17. Put epoxy glue on each bead and push it into a hole, so that about half of the bead is sticking up from the surface of the gourd. Allow all the beads to set.

18. Paint about 2 yards (1.8 m) of reed with black leather dye and allow it to dry. Soak the reed in water about five minutes, or until it becomes flexible.

19. Select two beads on the gourd for holding a strip of reed. Use the measuring tape to find out how far it is between the beads, adding an inch (2.5 cm) or more for the curvature of the reed. Use the craft knife to cut off a piece of reed slightly longer than this length. Gently bend the reed, and insert either end into the center of the two beads. Continue to add pieces of reed to create an "orbiting" effect.

beaded
MASK

materials & tools

Cured gourd (available at farmers' markets or craft stores)

Scouring pad, stainless steel or copper

Pencil

Dust mask

Small handheld drill

Drill bit, 3⁄32 inch (2.4 mm)

Small motorized cutting tool or small handheld power jigsaw

Grapefruit spoon

Coarse sandpaper

Fine-grit sandpaper

Black water-based spray enamel

Woodburner with large, rounded point

Rubber gloves

Several foam applicator brushes

Designer: DYAN PETERSON

Show off your most unusual beads on this gourd mask enlivened with a wild mane of wire hair.

instructions

materials & tools, continued

Cotton swabs

Medium brown leather dye

Black leather dye

Buckskin leather dye

Tan leather dye

Aqua green leather dye

Olive green felt pen

Hair dryer

Clear satin-finish spray lacquer

Wire cutters

18-gauge wire

Round-nose pliers

Assorted large and medium-sized beads

1. Remove the dirt and mold from the surface of the gourd with warm water and a scouring pad. Be careful not to scratch the skin of the gourd. Allow the gourd to dry.

2. Invert the gourd. Use the pencil to draw the shape of a mask onto the curved contours of the gourd (see figure 1 on page 38).

3. Put on the dust mask. Use the hand drill fitted with the small drill bit to drill a hole in the gourd just outside of the pencil line. Insert the cutting blade of your cutting tool or jigsaw in the hole, and cut to the pencil line. Continue sawing until you have cut along the entire line.

4. When you have finished cutting, remove the excess piece of gourd. Scrape away all of the pulp and seeds with the grapefruit spoon.

5. Once the gourd is clean, use the coarse sandpaper to smooth the inside walls. Sand again with the fine-grit sandpaper for a smooth, luscious interior.

6. Spray the inside of the gourd with the black water-based enamel. Allow to dry.

7. Use figure 1 on page 38 as a guide for drawing the lines for the face on the gourd, or make up your own design. Insert the large, rounded point in the woodburner, and heat up the tool by following the manufacturer's instructions. Following the

pencil lines of your design, outline the lines with the tip of the woodburner.

8. Cut out the right eye with the motorized cutting tool or jigsaw.

9. Put on the rubber gloves, and assemble the cotton swabs, foam brushes, dyes, felt pen, and hair dryer.

10. Use figure 1 on page 38 as a guide to apply the dyes to color various portions of the face with a sponge brush. Hasten the drying between applications by blowing dyed areas with the hair dryer. Use a cotton swab to add black dots of dye to the forehead.

11. To create a patterned headband on the forehead, woodburn or carve small squares, circles, and lines between the two woodburned lines.

12. After dyeing the area around the mouth with medium brown dye, sand it lightly with the fine-grit sandpaper to create an antique effect.

13. Spray a coat of clear satin-finish lacquer over the entire mask, and allow it to dry thoroughly.

14. Starting at the center of the right eye, ¼ inch (6 mm) from the edge of the mask, use the handheld drill to drill holes ½ inch (1.3 cm) apart around the crown until you reach the other eye.

15. Cut off a piece of wire about 8 inches (20.3 cm) long. Insert a long piece of wire into the second hole up on the left (leave the first hole blank). Attach the wire to the back of the mask by making several loops with round-nose pliers in the short end of the wire.

16. Place a bead on the long end of the wire. Push the free end of the wire into the next hole, and attach the end to the back as you did in step 15. Twist and curl the wire loosely with your fingers to create a hairlike effect.

17. Continue wiring beads to the edge of the mask in this way, varying the lengths of wire to look like hair. Leave the last hole on the right blank.

18. Stack beads onto a couple of short pieces of wire to simulate ear-rings, and twist the wire to hold the beads in place. Insert the ends of the wires into the blank holes. Fix the ends on the back of the mask.

19. Drill a hole in the top and bottom of the nose. Place a couple of beads on a short length of wire, insert the ends into the holes, and twist them together on the back to hold them in place.

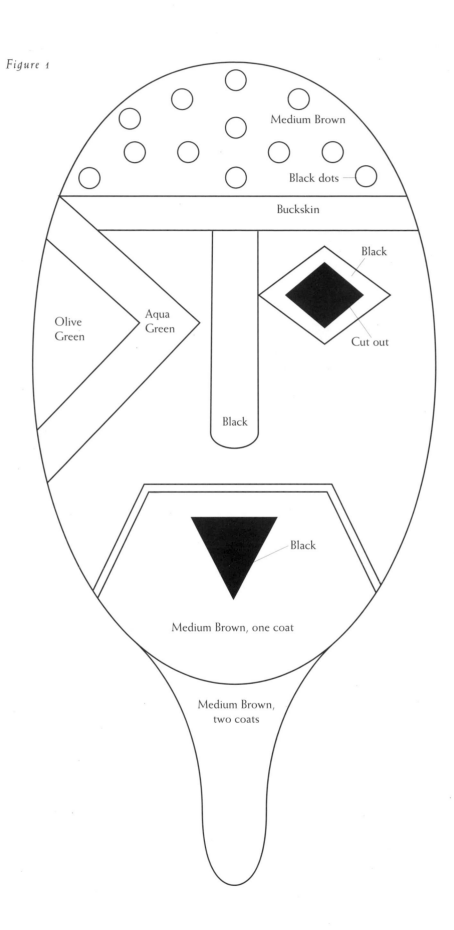

Figure 1

hanging GOURD VESSEL

Designer: DYAN PETERSON

materials & tools

Cured gourd with elongated shape and tall top, such as a kettle gourd (available at farmers' markets or craft stores)

Scouring pad, stainless steel or copper

Pencil

Dust mask

Electric drill

Drill bits, one ³⁄₃₂ inch (2.4 mm), one ³⁄₁₆ inch (4.8 mm)

Small motorized cutting tool or small handheld power jigsaw

Wood filler

Fine-grit sandpaper

Grapefruit spoon

Coarse sandpaper

Black water-based spray enamel

Complement the natural shape of a long-necked gourd with a scalloped edge laced with pine needles. Add linen cords strung with an array of beads to create a beautiful, functional vessel for any room of your home.

instructions

materials & tools, continued

Rubber gloves

Foam applicator brush

Buckskin leather dye

Medium brown leather dye

Aqua green leather dye

Cotton swabs

Mahogany leather dye

Hair dryer

Clear satin-finish spray lacquer

Gold marker

Brown waxed linen

Bunch of long leaf pine needles

Scissors

An assortment of large or medium-sized beads

1. Remove the dirt and mold from the surface of the gourd with warm water and a scouring pad. Be careful not to scratch the skin of the gourd. Allow the gourd to dry.

2. Orient the gourd upside down (with the neck at the bottom), since the neck is the part that you'll use as the vessel. With this in mind, use the pencil to draw a broad scalloped line around the neck, indicating the shape of the vessel below that line.

3. Put on the dust mask. Use the electric drill fitted with the ³⁄₁₆-inch (4.8 mm) drill bit to drill a hole about ½ inch (1.3 cm) above the cutting line.

4. Insert the cutting blade into the hole of your cutting tool or jigsaw, and saw down to the drawn line before sawing around the circumference of the gourd. Remove the top of the gourd.

5. If there are any cracks in the rim from sawing, fill them in with wood filler. After the filler dries, gently sand it smooth with the fine-grit sandpaper.

6. Scrape all of the pulp and seeds out of the gourd with the grapefruit spoon. Once the gourd is clean, use the coarse sandpaper to smooth the inside walls. Sand again with the fine-grit sandpaper for a smooth, luscious interior.

7. Spray the inside of the gourd with the black water-based enamel. Allow to dry.

8. Put on rubber gloves. Use the foam applicator brush to coat the outside of the gourd with the buckskin leather dye. If the color looks too yellow, add a few drops of the medium brown dye to the buckskin dye, and repaint it.

9. Mix the aqua green dye with a few drops of the medium brown dye to make an olive green dye. While the first coat of buckskin dye is still wet, dip a cotton swab into the olive green dye. Dab the olive green dye at random areas around the top of the rim. Allow the dyes to run together to simulate leaves.

10. While the olive green dye is still damp, dip another cotton swab into the mahogany dye. Make berry clusters on top of the leaves by dabbing clusters of dots over the olive green dye. Dry thoroughly with the hair dryer.

11. To seal the gourd and protect your work, apply a fine mist of clear satin-finish spray lacquer, and allow it to dry. Apply two or three more coats, drying the gourd thoroughly between each coat. (Be careful not to use too much lacquer in any one coat, or it will run and create drips.)

12. Use the gold marker to apply clusters of dots on top of the berries.

13. Use the drill and smaller drill bit to drill holes ¼ inch (6 mm) down from the rim and ½ inch (1.3 cm) apart all the way around the gourd.

14. Use waxed linen to lace through the holes and secure the pine needles to the rim of the gourd in small bunches, overlapping them as you go.

15. Cut off a 12-inch (30.5 cm) piece of waxed linen thread. Slide a bead onto the thread near one end, tie it off with a knot on either side to hold it in place, and then add several more beads in the same fashion, leaving the other half of the thread free.

16. Decide where you want to place the hanging beads on the rim, and loop the free end of the thread underneath the lacing at this point. Pull the free end of the thread through until the beads rest where you like. Add beads to the free end

of the thread in the same fashion. Add several more strands of beads around the perimeter of the vessel.

17. Cut off three pieces of waxed linen thread to assemble into a hanger for the vessel. Insert the end of each thread into a separate but adjacent hole at the top of the gourd on either side, and tie it securely inside.

18. Gather the loose ends of the thread and adjust them so that the gourd hangs level. Tie a knot at the top of the threads to prepare the gourd for hanging.

elegant DOOR TASSEL

Designer: SUSAN RIND

This moveable feast of beads and fringe adds a graceful touch to any entryway.

materials & tools

Two 48-inch (1.2 m) pieces of medium-diameter tigertail (flexible beading wire)

Round-nose pliers

4 silver crimp beads

Approximately 500 Japanese opalescent glass seed beads (size 4)

Approximately 700 seed beads of 2 colors (size 6)

Hollow wooden bell, approximately 2 inches (5.1 cm) long

Paintbrush

4 metallic paints (assorted neutral colors)

20-inch (50.8 cm) piece of twisted yarn fringe (neutral color)

Size 12 beading needle

Nylon beading thread

20-gauge stainless-steel wire, 48-inch (1.2 m) piece

Hot glue gun and glue sticks

Needle-nose pliers

12-gauge colored wire, 16-inch (40.6 cm) piece

Wire cutters

instructions

1. On each piece of flexible beading wire, use the round-nose pliers to place and flatten a crimp bead 4 inches (10.2 cm) from one end.

2. Set aside 33 size 4 glass seed beads, and 33 size 6 glass seed beads for later. From the remaining beads, feed size 4 and 6 beads onto the free end of both of the strands in a random pattern, leaving 4 inches (10.2 cm) of wire at the end. Place a crimp bead at this point and flatten it to hold the beads in place. Set these strands aside.

3. Paint the wooden bell with a mottled pattern of metallic colors achieved by layering. Allow two hours of drying time after the final color has been applied.

4. Lay the 20-inch (50.8 cm) piece of twisted yarn fringe on a flat surface. Beginning at one end, roll it up until approximately 2 inches (5.1 cm) of the fringe is rolled. Secure the roll at the top with stitches of beading thread.

5. Begin to thread beads of the same color onto the needle and thread until you create a 2¾-inch (7 cm) strand (or the length of your fringe).

6. Skipping the last bead you put on, feed the needle back through the strand of beads to return to the top of the fringe. Roll the yarn fringe up slightly before you secure it at the top with your thread.

7. Continue to add bead strands in alternating colors every ½ inch (1.3 cm)—rolling the fringe and securing the strands at the top as you go until it is completely rolled.

8. Push half of the stainless-steel wire through the top of the fringed roll to form a loop that is securely attached. Feed the wire through the center of the wooden bell, and pull the fringe up tightly into the opening until the excess wire comes out of the top.

9. Use the glue gun to fill the hollow top part of the bell with glue. Allow the glue to set for two hours to create a secure seal.

10. Use round-nose pliers to twist the excess wire in free-form loops to cover the top of the bell, adding beads in random order during the looping process.

11. When about 4 inches (10.2 cm) of wire remains on both ends, use the pliers to grip and twist these wires and the ends of the bead strands (created in steps 1 and 2) together. Use the remainder of the wire to make loops to hide the twisted ends of the wire.

12. Feed the 33 size 4 glass beads from step 2 onto the 12-gauge colored wire, and wrap it around the bell near the top just beneath the wire creation. Twist the ends to tighten around the bell, clip off the excess wire, and hide the ends under the beads. Repeat the process using the size 6 seed beads, and attach them just above the Japanese beads.

13. Tie a knot in the beaded strands at the top of the bell to create a loop for hanging.

lovely
FRINGED TABLECLOTH

Designer: CHARLI TRAYLOR

A delicate beaded fringe creates visual interest all the way around the table.

materials & tools

70-inch (177.8 cm) round tablecloth

2 inch-long (5.1 cm) piece of string

Scissors

Colored chalk

Nylon beading thread

Size 10 beading needle

2–3 hanks of seed beads (size 11)

200 fire-polished beads (4 mm)

Fire-polished teardrops with vertical holes (7 x 5 mm)

Beading glue

instructions

1. Lay your tablecloth wrong side up on a flat surface.

2. With the string and chalk, make small marks 2 inches (5.1 cm) apart all the way around the edge of the tablecloth. Turn the table-cloth over.

3. Cut a piece of beading thread 3 yards (2.7 m) long.

4. Push a threaded needle through the tablecloth ¼ inch (6 mm) above the edge at the first chalk mark. Leave a 3-inch (7.6 cm) tail. Tie off the thread with a knot on the back of the tablecloth.

5. String on 25 seed beads, one 4 mm fire-polished bead, and 25 seed beads.

6. Push your needle in ¼ inch (6 mm) from the edge at the next chalk mark (figure 1). Take your needle back down through the last bead you exited.

7. String on 24 seed beads, one 4 mm fire-polished bead, and 25 seed beads.

8. Repeat steps 6 and 7, working your way around the entire table-cloth until only one section remains unbeaded. On this section of thread, string on 24 seed beads, one 4 mm fire-polished bead, and 24 seed beads. Go up through the very first bead you strung in step 5, and take a stitch through the tablecloth.

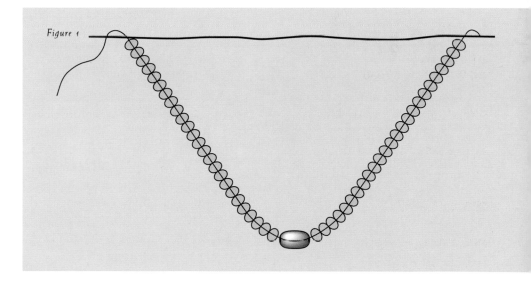

Figure 1

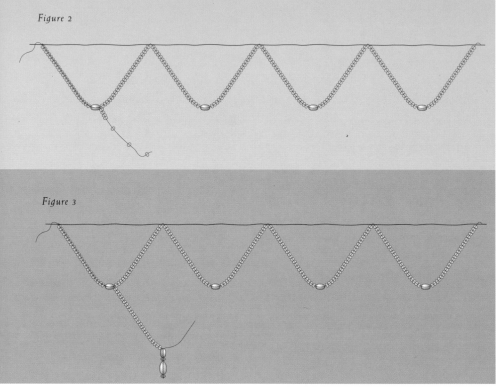

Figure 2

Figure 3

9. Go back down through this bead and the subsequent beads, threading through the beads below until your thread comes out of the 4 mm fire-polished bead (figure 2). (In other words, you've made one complete revolution around the tablecloth and now you're making a second in the same direction.)

10. Thread on 25 seed beads, one 4 mm fire-polished bead, one seed bead, one 7 x 5 mm fire-polished teardrop, and one seed bead.

11. Go back up through the teardrop, skipping the last seed bead you put on. Continue threading up through the seed bead and the 4 mm fire-polished bead. Pull your thread tight (figure 3).

12. Thread on 25 more seed beads, and take your needle

through the next 4 mm fire-polished bead in the first row.

13. Repeat this process to add another level of fringe all the way around the tablecloth.

14. After your last stitch, go through the 4 mm fire-polished bead and the 25 seed beads above it. You should end up at the edge of your tablecloth.

15. Take your needle back through the tablecloth and tie a knot in the thread. Dab a drop of glue on the knot and pass the needle back down through five seed beads before cutting the thread.

16. Thread your needle onto the 3-inch (7.6 cm) tail from step 4. Pass through several seed beads and trim your thread close.

window screen
LIGHT CATCHER

Designer: SANDIE ABEL

materials
& tools

Photocopy of template
(page 49)

8½ x 11-inch (21.6 x 27.9 cm)
piece of fiberglass window
screen (available at hardware
stores)

Light-colored dressmaker's
pencil

Size 12 beading needle

White nylon beading thread

Brown color-lined seed beads
(size 11)

Transparent white seed beads
(size 11)

31 pale green matte glass leaf
beads with hole at base

37 pale pink matte glass flower
beads with hole at base

Scissors

Black seed beads (size 11)

A piece of window screen holds a beautiful glass bead wreath inspired by the subtle hues of early spring.

instructions

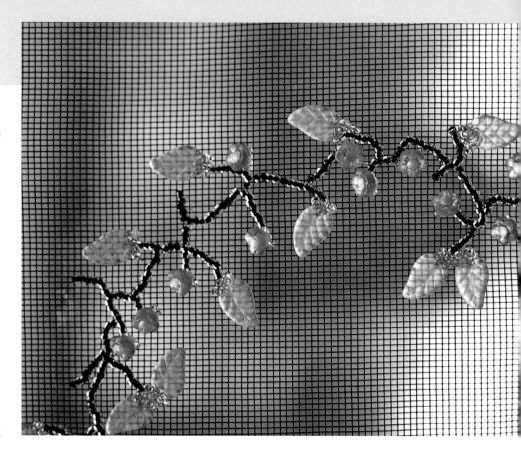

1. Place the photocopy of the template on a flat surface with the fiberglass window screen centered on top of it. Use a pencil to lightly trace the lines indicating the branches (the brown portions on the finished piece) onto the screen.

2. Thread the beading needle with white thread. Pull the thread through at the tip of one of the branches, and leave a 5-inch (12.7 cm) tail. Sew on the brown seed beads with a running stitch (add a few beads and then anchor them by backstitching through the last few before moving on the next line of beads [see page 27]). Add lines of connecting beads with a running stitch until you complete the branches. When you finish a line of beads, tie off the thread and hide the knot in the beads as described on page 14.

3. Use one of the following techniques to add either a leaf or flower, using the template as a guide for placement:

a. To add a leaf bead, pull the thread through on the screen where you plan to affix the bead, and string on the bead. Add four transparent white seed beads. Go down through the screen right beneath the bottom tip of the leaf. Come back up through the leaf's hole, and then put on three beads before pushing the needle back through the screen to the left of the first line of beads. Repeat this step to add three more beads to the right side of the first line of beads (the beads will form a crow's foot). Secure the bead configuration on the back with a few hidden stitches. Run the thread through the brown beads until you get to the next flower or leaf.

b. To add a flower, pull the thread through at the point where you plan to affix the bead, and pick up one transparent white seed bead, one flower bead, and one more white seed bead. Pull the thread to the back of the screen, and secure it with a few hidden stitches. Run the thread through all three beads again to secure them before running the thread through the brown beads to the next flower or leaf.

4. Finish the edge of the screen with a continuous line of black seed beads attached with a running stitch.

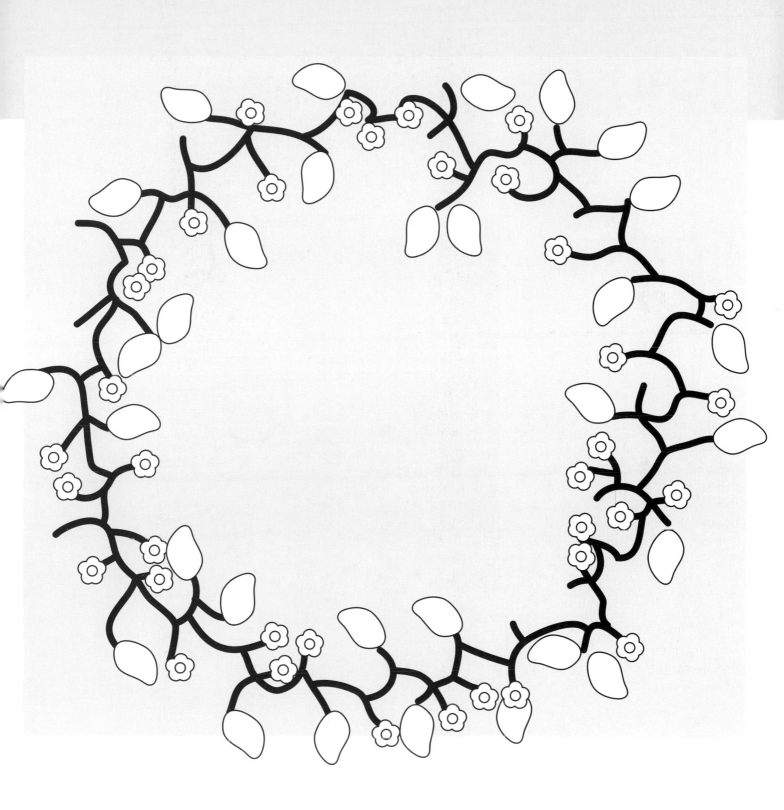

bone BEAD BOXES

Designer: TERRY TAYLOR

A declaration of "less is more"—these beautiful boxes combine the simplest of materials in a conscious, artistic manner.

materials & tools

Papier-mâché boxes
(available at craft stores)

Pencil

Assortment of bone beads

Tapestry needle

Nylon beading thread

Nail polish with nylon
(non-acetone)

instructions

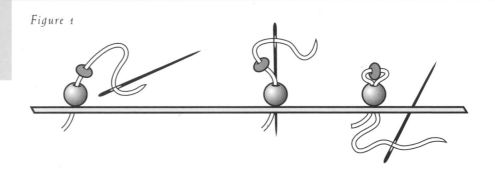

Figure 1

1. Arrange beads in a design of your choice on top of the boxes. Mark the position of each of the beads with a light pencil mark underneath the bead. Remove the beads.

2. Punch the tapestry needle through each of the marks.

3. Thread the tapestry needle with beading thread, knot the end and push it up through the back of the lid to the front at one of the holes.

4. Thread a bead (or beads) onto the thread, and push the needle back down through the lid of the box. To stack one smaller bead on top of a larger one, thread on the two beads before inserting the needle back through the larger bead, skipping the smaller bead (figure 1).

5. Move to the adjacent hole, and bring the thread back through to the front before stringing on the next bead. Continue to add beads in this fashion. When finished, tie the thread off on the back of the lid, and paint on nail polish to secure the thread.

dragonfly
WINDCHIME

Designer: HEATHER HORNE

A dancing cascade of beads and bells tinkles with the smallest breeze on this fanciful windchime.

materials & tools

Wire cutters

Measuring tape

3 yards (2.7 m) of 16-gauge brass-plated or copper wire

10 yards (9 m) of 28-gauge brass-plated or copper wire

Round-nose pliers

5 yards (4.5 m) of lightweight braided monofilament

1 hank Czech seed beads (size 11)

1 tube Czech seed beads (size 6)

12 glass flower beads (10 mm)

36 glass leaf beads with holes through their bases (8 x 6 mm)

16 brass jingle bells, ½ inch (1.3 cm) each

8 inches (20.3 cm) of 22-gauge brass-plated or copper wire

1 rice bead (7 x 4 mm)

7 rondell beads (6 mm)

6 crow beads (6 mm)

1 round bead (12 mm)

1 tube clear or lined seed beads (size 11)

24–32 brass jump rings (5 mm)

10–16 brass dragonflies, 1 x ½ inch (2.5 x 1.3 cm) each

8 inches (20.3 cm) of 22-gauge brass-plated or copper wire

Round-nosed pliers

1 rice bead (7 x 4 mm)

7 rondell beads (6 mm)

6 crow beads (6 mm)

1 round bead (12 mm)

1 tube clear or lined seed beads, (size 11)

24–32 brass jump rings (5 mm)

10–16 brass dragonflies, 1 x ½ inch (2.5 x 1.3 cm) each

instructions

1. Cut off 2 yards (1.8 m) of 16-gauge wire. Bend the wire into a circle with a 6-inch (15.2 cm) diameter. Wrap the end of the tail of the wire around the circle to hold its shape.

2. To make the hanger for the windchime, cut off a 2-foot (60 cm) section of the 16-gauge wire. Wrap the wire tightly with 28-gauge wire, leaving 3 inches (7.6 cm) unwrapped at each end.

4. Fold the wrapped wire in half. Twist the wire together twice about 2 inches (5.1 cm) below the fold to form a loop. Insert the end of the pliers into the loop, and push the wire apart above the twist to form an opening.

5. Pull the rest of the wire into the shape of an open triangle with the ends about 6 inches (15.2 cm) apart. Tightly wrap the bottom unwrapped portions of wire around the wrapped circle on opposite sides.

6. String the following beads onto the monofilament in this order: 20 size 11 seed beads, one size 6 seed bead, one glass flower, one size 6 seed bead, and 20 size 11 seed beads.

7. Repeat the pattern of one size 6 seed bead and 20 size 11 seed beads four times. Add one size 6 seed bead, one glass leaf bead, and one size 6 seed bead.

8. Continue stringing 20 size 11 seed beads, one size 6 seed bead, and 14 size 11 seed beads. Place the brass bell onto the strand next, and string on 6 more size 11 seed beads. Skip over the last 12 seed beads you put on (with the brass bell in the middle), and thread the monofilament up through the next seed bead to form a loop at the bottom of the strand.

9. Tie a hidden knot (see page 14), and thread the monofilament through about an inch (2.5 cm) of beads before cutting it. Tie the top end of the strand to the wire circle.

10. Repeat steps 6 through 9 to create 15 more strands, altering each one slightly by varying the placement of the leaf bead. Tie each strand onto the wire circle 1¼ inches (3.2 cm) apart.

11. Cut two sections of 28-gauge wire, each 70 inches (177.8 cm) long. Tie a knot 3½ inches (8.9 cm) from the end of each wire. String both wires with the following pattern: 6 inches (15.2 cm) of size

11 seed beads, one glass leaf bead, and 6 inches (15.2 cm) of size 11 seed beads. Tie off the wire at the top, immediately after the last bead. Tie a knot at each end of the wire immediately after the last bead to keep the beads from falling off.

12. Wind a section of wire around your hand to make it more compact for wrapping, and begin tightly wrapping the wire circle where the hanger attaches. Wrap the wire tightly around half of the circle to the other hanger. Wrap the second piece of wire around the other half of the circle.

13. To make the dragonfly, fold the 8-inch (20.3 cm) piece of 22-gauge wire in half. With the tip of the round-nose pliers, roll the folded end into a small loop.

14. Stack the rice bead, one rondell, and one crow bead onto the 28-gauge wire. Alternate one rondell and one crow bead until you have used all of them.

15. Add the 12 mm round bead for the dragonfly's head, and trim the wire ¼ inch (6 mm) from it.

16. With the tip of the round-nose pliers, roll the wire over into another small loop. If you want your dragonfly to have antennae, pull the loops apart slightly.

17. Cut a 2-foot (60 cm) piece of 28-gauge wire for the wings. String 1 foot (30 cm) of the clear size 11 seed beads onto the wire, leaving 6 inches (15.2 cm) of wire at either end.

18. Wrap one end of the wire underneath the first bead below the dragonfly's head, and count out 40 size 11 seed beads. Fold the wire in half and count 40 more seed beads. Push the rest of the beads ¼ inch (6 mm) down the wire.

19. Wrap the free section of wire over the same place you started and take the wire over to the other side of the dragonfly. Make three more wings exactly like the first, placing two wings on each side of the dragonfly's body.

19. When you have completed all four wings, use the excess wire to wrap around the dragonfly's "neck" at least twice to secure the wings. Then trim the wire. Shape your dragonfly's wings by pulling them slightly apart, just enough so it looks like there are two bottom wings and two top wings.

20. Cut a 1-foot (30 cm) piece of monofilament, and tie a square knot around your dragonfly just above the wings. Attach the other end to the bottom of the loop on your hanger.

21. To put the dragonfly accents on your strands, attach a jump ring to the dragonfly (see page 15), and close it completely. Attach another jump ring to the one you just put on, but before closing it, place it on a beaded strand.

22. Repeat step 21, spacing out the brass dragonflies until you have used them all.

illuminate

Light up the
rooms of your
home with the
beauty of a
candlestick
wrapped in wire
and beads or
the dazzling
shimmer of a
beaded valance.

embellished
CANDLESTICK

Designer: SUSAN RIND

materials & tools

Wire cutters

20-gauge stainless-steel wire, approximately 3 yards (2.7 m)

12-inch-high (30.5 cm) metal candlestick

5 oval lampwork beads (¾ inch [1.9 cm])

Approximately 100 faceted beads in assorted colors (4 to 10 mm)

Needle-nose pliers

Round-nose pliers

10–15 large stone nugget beads (we used Russian amber beads)

12-inch-long (30.5 cm) piece of tigertail (flexible beading wire)

3 silver crimp beads

2 lampwork teardrop-shaped beads (¾ inch [1.9 cm])

This cool metal candlestick contrasts with the warmth of glistening lampwork beads and stone nuggets.

instructions

1. Cut off a 60-inch (1.5 m) piece of stainless-steel wire. Wrap the wire twice around the base of the candlestick, leaving 8 inches (20.3 cm) free on the end to finish later.

2. Feed beads onto the longer wire, alternating four of the five oval lampwork beads with small faceted beads. Fill enough wire with beads to circle the base of the candlestick. Use pliers to help you twist the two wires together to hold the beads in place.

3. Fill the 8-inch (20.3 cm) shorter wire with a stone nugget and several faceted beads. Use round-nose pliers to twist and loop the wire in a decorative fashion on the front to hold the beads in place. Hide the end in the wires that are already in place.

4. Thread 40 to 50 faceted beads of various sizes on the wire, and spiral the wire up the stem of the candlestick. Wrap the bare wire around the next juncture on your candlestick.

5. String on more nuggets and faceted beads, and circle the juncture. To secure the beads, wrap the bare wire tightly a couple of times.

6. Continue this process of adding beads and looping the wires as you move up the candlestick. When you've traversed the height of it, loop the wire in small circles on the front to secure the beads, and hide the end behind the ones that are in place.

7. Cut off a 4-inch-long (10.2 cm) piece of flexible beading wire. Bend the wire in half, and feed it through one of the small looped circles of wire that you created at the top of the candlestick in step 6. Onto the doubled wire, feed a nugget, the last oval lampwork bead, a faceted 8 mm bead, and a silver crimp

bead. Flatten the crimp bead with pliers, and cut off any remaining wire to form a hanging tassel.

8. Thread the other piece of beading wire through the beads at the base of the candlestick, and tie a hidden knot in the wire to hold it in place. Feed the following beads onto each of the strands to create beaded tassels: three faceted beads, one teardrop, one faceted bead, and a silver crimp bead. Flatten the crimp beads with the pliers.

wire mesh
CANDLE SHADE

Designer: BRENDA L. SPITZER

materials
& tools

Thin metal ruler

Water soluble marking pen

16 x 20-inch (40.6 x 50.8 cm) sheet brass decorative mesh (8 mesh)

Wire cutters

Hammer

26-gauge brass wire

26-gauge tinned copper wire

40 green seed beads, size 5

35 yellow seed beads, size 5

60 silver-lined crystal seed beads

Needle-nose pliers

3-inch (7.6 cm) triangular candle

Candle and flame are encased in brass mesh decorated with dancing flowers and beads.

instructions

1. Use the ruler and marking pen to mark a 16 x 9-inch (40.6 x 22.9 cm) rectangle on the brass decorative mesh. Cut out the rectangle.

2. To create smooth folded edges on the brass mesh rectangle, place the mesh on a hard work surface. Place the ruler ½ inch (1.3 cm) from the edge of the mesh. Fold the edge over the ruler, and gently hammer it flat. Repeat this process around the entire perimeter of the rectangle.

3. To create the triangular shape of the candle shade, place the ruler 5 inches (12.7 cm) from one short edge of the mesh (parallel to the edges), and bend the mesh to an approximate 45° angle. Repeat at the other short edge of the mesh. Bring the folded edges of the mesh together.

4. Cut a 20-inch (50.8 cm) length of the brass wire. At the top corner of the triangular shade where the two edges join, insert an inch (2.5 cm) of wire through the mesh, and wrap this short end of the wire around the longer wire to hold it in place.

5. Whipstitch the edges of the shade together by hand. At the bottom, twist the wire around itself and trim it.

6. To decorate the top and bottom edges of the candle shade, cut two 36-inch (91.4 cm) lengths of tinned copper wire. Begin on the top edge and insert one end of the wire in the corner to secure it as you did in step 4.

7. Create scallops by loosely stitching wire through the mesh from front to back at 1-inch (2.5 cm) intervals, threading a green or yellow seed bead on each scallop

as you go. Decorate the bottom edge with a line of beaded scallops an inch (2.5 cm) from the bottom.

8. To make six eight-pointed stars to add as decorative embellishment, use tinned copper wire, green beads, yellow beads, and silver-lined beads. To make a star, cut off a 36-inch (91.4 cm) length of wire. Bend the wire eight times, accordion style, at 3-inch (7.6 cm) intervals, threading a green or yellow bead at each bend (figure 1). Twist tightly, three times, below each bead to hold it in place (figure 2, next page).

Figure 1

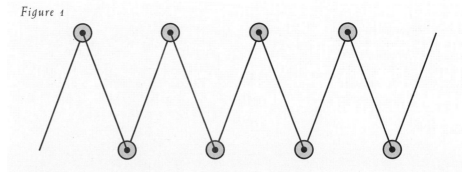

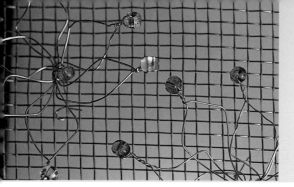

9. Pinch the folds of the wire together and grasp at the center. Wrap the long end of the wire tightly around the center twice (figure 3).

Figure 2

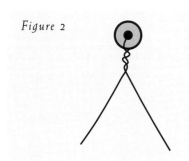

Figure 3

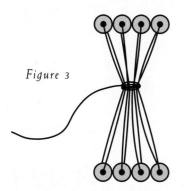

Thread a crystal bead on the wire, and wrap it tightly twice more. Trim the ends of the wire to approximately 2 inches (5.1 cm).

10. To separate the wires into eight spokes extending from the center of the star, insert the needle-nose pliers between each of the folded wires at the center of the spoke. Gently open the pliers to bend the spokes into a diamond shape (figure 4). Set aside the six stars.

11. To make nine six-pointed stars, you'll use brass wire, green beads, yellow beads, and crystal beads. For each star, cut a 30-inch (76.2 cm) length of wire. Bend the wire six times, accordion style, at

3-inch (7.6 cm) intervals, threading a crystal bead at each bend. Twist tightly, three times, below each bead.

12. Bring the folds of wire together and grasp at the center. Wrap the long end of wire tightly around the center two times. Thread a green or yellow bead onto the wire, and wrap tightly twice. Trim the ends of the wire to approximately 2 inches (5.1 cm).

13. Follow step 10 to separate the spokes with the needle-nose pliers.

14. Attach two eight-pointed stars and three six-pointed stars to each side of the candle shade by inserting the ends through the mesh and twisting the wire together tightly inside. Trim the ends of the wire.

15. Place the candle inside the shade.

Figure 4

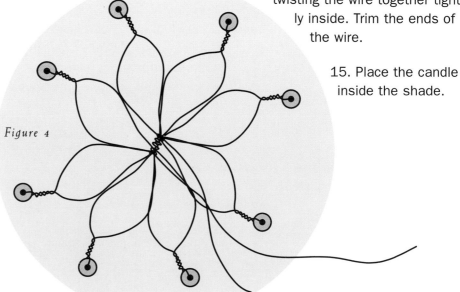

galactic
CURTAIN TIEBACKS

Designer: SANDIE ABEL

These beautiful tiebacks adorned with hanging stars will light up your living room or bedroom.

materials & tools

For two tiebacks:

30 inches (76.2 cm) of metallic ribbon, 1½ inches (3.8 cm) wide

Scissors

Fine sewing needle

Black quilting thread

2 yards (1.8 m) of gold braided trim

10 feet (3 m) of thin, gold metallic cord

2 large star beads

34 small star beads

instructions

1. Fold the metallic ribbon in half, and cut it into two 15-inch (38.1 cm) pieces. Turn the ends of each piece under ⅜ inch (9.5 mm), and hem by hand with small stitches of the quilting thread.

2. Cut the gold braided trim in half. Turn the ends under, and tack them into place with the thread to prevent fraying.

3. Cut the gold metallic cord into 8-inch (20.3 cm) lengths. Fold one of the pieces of cord in half to create a loop at the top, and position it on the back side of the metallic ribbon (from step 1) near one end along the bottom of it. Sew the top of the loop into place, catching about an inch (2.5 cm) of cord along the bottom of the ribbon so that the ends hang apart. Sew another looped cord into place on the other end of the ribbon in the same fashion.

4. Between the two loops that you've attached, place a loop in the center of the strip, followed by two on each side of the center. (Allow the ends of the loops to hang at different lengths.) Repeat this process on the other piece of metallic ribbon.

5. Place one end of a piece of the gold braided trim at the center of the lower edge of the metallic ribbon in a lengthwise position. (Line up the bottom edge of the trim with the bottom edge of the ribbon.) Attach this end with small stitches. Position the other end of the trim next to this end in the same manner, so that the two ends face one another. Sew it into place.

6. Tack the lower edge of the trim to the lower edge of the ribbon with small stitches, working from the center to the ends. Take a few extra stitches at the ends to make sure the trim is attached tightly. Then sew the upper edge of the trim to the ribbon.

7. Leave a 2-inch (5.1 cm) loop on either end, and sew the other half of the trim to the upper edge of the ribbon along the top. To make this process easier, start in the center, and work toward each end. (There's no need to sew the lower edge of the braid down on this top edge.)

8. Repeat steps 5 through 7 on the other tieback.

9. Sew a large star over the lower edge of each tieback at the join of the trim in the center.

10. Sew a line of three small stars over the edges of the hems on the front side of each tieback to hide the seams.

11. To add the stars to the ends of the cords, thread the needle and push the thread through one of the cords about ⅜ inch (9.5 mm) from the bottom. Place a star bead on the needle, and push the thread through the cord again. Run the thread back through twice to secure the star. Knot off and clip the thread close. Add stars to all of the cords in this fashion.

bejeweled TEA LIGHT HOLDER

materials & tools

22-gauge copper wire,
2 yards plus 6 inches (2 m)

Wire cutters

Perforated metal tea light holder in shape of potted flower or other shape that lends itself to embellishment

Needle-nose pliers

Round-nose pliers

20-gauge stainless-steel wire,
40-inch-long (1 m) piece

Approximately 50 assorted faceted beads (8 to 12 mm)

Add dimension to the simple outline of a metal tea light holder with a randomly wrapped center of wire and beads.

Designer: SUSAN RIND

instructions

1. Cut the copper wire into two 40-inch (1 m) lengths.

2. Push a piece of the copper wire through one of the perforations in the tea light holder, and anchor it on the back by looping the end of the wire so that it doesn't pull out of the perforation.

3. Weave the copper wire in and out of alternating holes on the periphery of the flower (or adapt this technique to another shape).

4. Pull the other piece of copper wire from the back through the center of the flower or other shape, and attach it to the back as you did in step 2.

5. Use the pliers to help you loop the copper wire around and around in the center of the flower.

6. Pull the stainless-steel wire through the center, and anchor it to the back with a loop. String a group of beads onto the wire, and then loop it under and over the central mass of copper wire. Continue to add groups of beads in this fashion, looping the wire as you go until you like the results.

7. Hide the wire end in the decorative loops.

LAMPSHADE
with seed bead fringe

Designer: DEBI SCHMITZ

This elegant lampshade is adorned with a fringe of metallic seed and bugle beads.

materials & tools

Two size 12 beading needles or appliqué needles

Nylon beading thread in color that complements shade

Metallic seed and bugle beads to complement color of shade

Measuring tape

Round lampshade in color of your choice

Small tube of beading glue

instructions

1. Thread two needles with 1 yard (.9 m) of beading thread. Tie knots in the end of each thread.

2. Thread one seed bead, one bugle bead, and one seed bead onto a needle, and pull until the knot catches. Run the other needle through the beads from the opposite direction, and pull until the knot catches (figure 1).

3. Thread one seed bead, one bugle bead, and one seed bead onto each needle. After completing this, thread one more sequence of beads (seed, bugle, and seed) onto the left needle (figure 2). Run the right needle through this last sequence of beads from the other direction. The beads will form a box .

4. You'll now have two lines of thread coming out of the box in opposite directions. On the left thread, add a seed bead, a bugle bead, two seed beads, a bugle bead, and a seed bead. On the right thread, add on a seed bead, bugle bead, and a seed bead.

5. Snug the beads up by pulling on the thread, and run the right thread back through the last three beads (seed, bugle, and seed) that you put on the left thread (figure 3). (The threads will be coming out of the bead sequence on opposite sides.)

6. Pull the thread up tight so that the line of beads forms the fourth side of the box. Continue to add

beads in this way until you have a long enough fringe to run around the bottom edge of the lampshade just above the hemline.

7. Make another square sequence of beads to fit around the top of the lampshade just under the hemline.

8. To add dangles to the boxes, begin by pulling a knotted thread through the right bottom seed bead

Figure 1

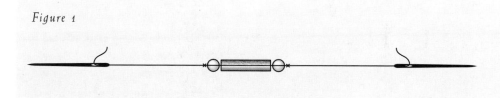

Figure 2

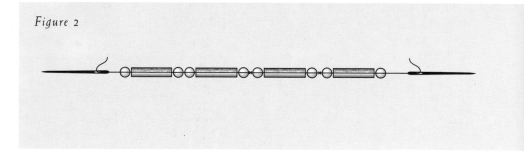

on one of the boxes. Thread the following onto the needle: one seed bead, one bugle bead, four seed beads, one bugle bead, and five seed beads.

9. Skip the five seed beads that you put on last, and then thread the needle back up through the final bugle bead and three of the seed beads. (The five seed beads will form a circular loop at the bottom.)

Figure 3   Figure 4

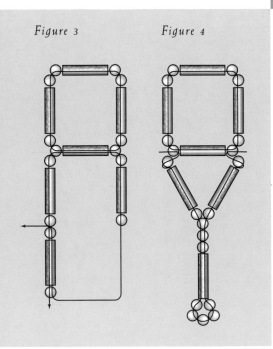

10. String on one seed bead, a bugle bead, and a seed bead to complete the dangle (figure 4). Run the needle through the next seed bead up (on the original strand), and pull the thread up tight. Come back through the next seed bead to the left on the bottom of the original strand of boxes, and repeat this process to form the next dangle. Continue adding fringe across the bottom of the boxes until you've gone all the way across the strand.

11. Attach the bead strand to the lampshade ¼ inch (6 mm) above the bottom edge of the shade with a needle and beading thread. To do this, run the beading needle through several beads before punching the needle through the lampshade. Sew down the corner of every third box, alternating top and bottom corners. The thread on the inside of the lampshade will form a zigzag. Use the same method to attach the square sequence of beads that you made in step 7 to the top of the lampshade.

12. Glue small clusters of remaining beads onto the lampshade in a random fashion.

embellished
METAL FINIAL

materials & tools

20-gauge stainless-steel wire, 48 inches (1.2 m) long

Metal finial with open prongs

Needle-nose pliers

About 40 faceted beads in assorted colors (4–8 mm)

2 oblong colored glass beads, 1¼ inches (3.2 cm) each

2 flat, round metal beads, ½ inch (1.3 cm) each

Flat piece of cane glass

A taut strand of beads in the center of this finial transforms it into an object worthy of display on an elegant lamp or a curtain rod.

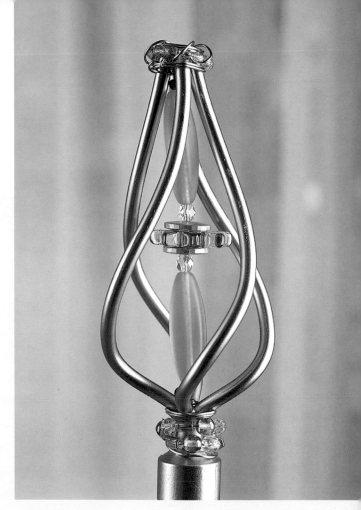

Designer: SUSAN RIND

instructions

1. Wrap the stainless-steel wire twice around the bottom of the finial at the crease, leaving a tail of 12 inches (30.5 cm). Loop the tail of the wire over on itself a couple of times to secure it with a twist.

2. Feed enough assorted faceted beads onto the 12-inch-long (30.5 cm) wire tail to circle the base twice. Wrap the leftover wire around the base and hide the end behind the beads.

3. String a progression of beads onto the remaining wire that is long enough to span the center of the finial. (We used one oblong bead, one faceted bead, one metal bead, the flat piece of cane glass, one metal bead, one faceted bead, and one oblong bead.)

4. Loop the wire around the top of the finial to secure and tighten it, leaving 12 inches (30.5 cm) of wire free. Feed assorted beads onto the wire as you did in step 2, and wrap the top of the finial. Curl and loop the end of the wire in and out of the last beads to secure it.

dressed up
VOTIVE HOLDER

Designer: SUSAN RIND

Watch the relection of a candle's light on the stem of this embellished candleholder.

materials & tools

Glass votive holder with tall stem

22-gauge electrical copper wire, 7-strand twist, 40-inch-long (1 m) piece

20-gauge stainless-steel wire, 60 inches (1.5 m) long

Flat-nose pliers

Needle-nose pliers

Assorted faceted beads (8–12 mm)

instructions

1. Begin at the base of the votive holder, and wrap the end of the copper wire around the base several times before wrapping it in a spiral up the stem of the holder. Circle the top of the stem several times to hold the wire in place.

2. Pull 4 inches (10.2 cm) of the strands apart on each end. Use the pliers to create decorative loops and flourishes.

3. Twist the stainless-steel wire around a portion of the copper wire at the base of the holder to secure it.

4. Feed assorted beads onto the wire, and then wind the strand up the stem, following the same path as the copper wire.

5. At the top of the stem, loop the stainless-steel wire through a portion of the copper wire, and string on another series of beads. Twist and wind the beaded wire around the top in a decorative fashion. Hold the beads and wire in place with circular loops.

6. Hide the end of the wire behind the beads.

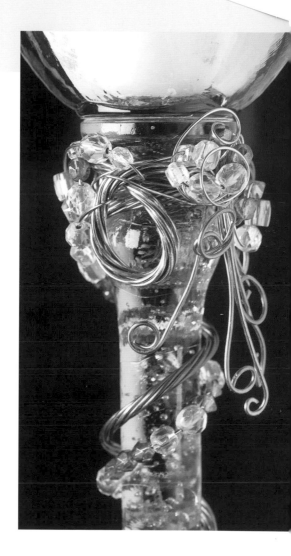

beaded
VALANCE

Designer: LINDA KALWEIT

Seemingly weightless strands of beads create an ever-changing curtain of light in a window. This project will require a lot of time, but it is simple to make.

materials & tools

3 small bowls

3 colors of size 8 seed beads (1 hank or 80 grams per color)

2 colors of size 6 seed beads (30 grams per color)

2 colors of 4 x 4 mm cubes (50 grams per color)

Size 5 drops (10 grams)

5 different shapes or colors of faceted beads (400 pieces)

6 mm round beads in one color (50 pieces)

4 mm discs (beads with a vertical hole) in one color (130 pieces)

instructions

materials & tools, *continued*

Size 5 triangles in one color
(20 grams)

Size 8 triangles in one color
(50 grams)

40 yards (36 m) of medium-weight
braided monofilament

Nail polish with nylon
(non-acetone)

Scissors

Measuring tape

80 crimp beads

80 charms

Needle-nose pliers

28-inch-long (71.1 cm)
curtain rod

1. Mix beads of a similar size
in each of the three bowls.

2. Coat the end of the braided
monofilament with the nail polish.
After it dries, use the scissors to
trim the end into a point.

3. Thread beads from each of the
bowls onto the monofilament,
mixing shapes and sizes.

4. When you have strung a length
of beads several yards long, measure off 29 inches (73.7 cm) of
beads, and then leave 3 inches
(7.6 cm) of blank monofilament
for crimping and hanging them
(figure 1). Cut the monofilament
at this point.

5. On each end of the strand,
string a crimp bead, add a charm,
and thread the end back through
the crimp.

6. Pull the monofilament tight,
and close the crimp with the
needle-nose pliers. Cut the monofilament close to the crimp bead.
Repeat on the other end.

7. Follow this same process until
you've created 40 strands.

8. Drape each strand at its mid-
point on the curtain rod, allowing
the blank area of monofilament to
cover the top of the rod so that
beads hang down on either side.

Figure 1

Jeweled LAMP PULL

Designer: KELLY LIGHTNER

materials & tools

1 crimp bead

1 yard (.9 m) of tigertail (flexible beading wire) (.012 or .018 diameter)

Assorted small and large beads

1 ball chain connector (available at craft or bead stores)

Teardrop-shaped bead with vertical hole

Needle-nose pliers

This simple accent gives new life to a plain lamp.

instructions

1. String the crimp bead onto the tigertail.

2. Choose a small bead that fits inside the ball chain connector, and add it to the wire beneath the crimp bead.

3. String an assortment of small and large beads in a design that pleases you to make up a pull of a length that suits your lamp.

4. String on the teardrop-shaped bead, followed by a small bead.

5. Skipping over the small bead, thread the wire back through all of the beads and through the crimp.

6. Pull the piece tight and leave a space between the top bead and the crimp bead.

7. Squeeze the crimp closed with pliers, and trim the wire.

8. Snap the crimp bead and the first bead of the piece into the ball chain connector.

9. Attach the pull to your lamp with the other end of the ball chain connector.

celebrate

Recognize special days with gorgeous beaded cutlery or made-for-a-soiree sparkling glasses.

opulent
SERVING PIECES

Designer: SUSAN RIND

Czech and Austrian crystals adorn the handles of these glorious serving pieces that will impress even the toniest guests.

materials & tools

4 yards (3.6 m) of 20-gauge stainless-steel wire

Wire cutters

Knife and cake server set, silver or stainless-steel base with acrylic handle (ridged handles are recommended)

Round-nose pliers

About 20 size 6 matte white seed beads

About 20 4 mm matte white cubes

Assorted crystal beads in various sizes, types, and colors (Czech, Austrian, and Japanese)

instructions

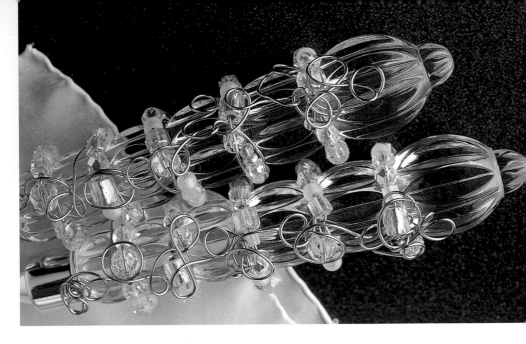

1. Cut two pieces of stainless-steel wire, each 71 inches (1.8 m) long.

2. Leaving a wire tail of about 3 inches (7.6 cm), wrap the wire in the groove of one of the utensil handles where the silver or stainless steel joins the acrylic handle.

3. On the front of the handle at the seam, use the needle-nose pliers to twist the short end of the wire around the long end once. Use the round-nose pliers to randomly loop the short end around the twist to hide it, and then stretch the wire down the handle about ½ inch (1.3 cm) before looping it tightly around the handle. (If your serving pieces have ridges, secure the wire in the first ridge.)

4. On the remaining wire, feed on approximately 15 seed beads, cubes, and crystals until you have a strand long enough to circle the handle. Loop the wire and beads tightly over the piece of wire that you just placed on the handle, and twist the wire into a circular loop on top of the beads to hold it in place. Use the round-nose pliers to loop and curl wire to get to the next ridge or position on the handle.

5. Repeat steps 3 and 4, continuing to add beads and looped wire until you traverse the length of the handle (moving from ridge to ridge or down the handle by ½-inch [1.3 cm] increments). Loop and curl the final strand of wire to hold the beads in place.

6. Repeat this process to add wire and beads to the other utensil.

(Note: After use, carefully hand wash the set in mild detergent before drying them with a clean cotton cloth.)

lone star COASTERS

materials & tools

Tapestry needle

Recycled rubber coasters in shape of stars or other motif

26-gauge copper wire

Wire cutters

Needle-nose pliers

Mixed seed beads in colors of your choice

instructions

1. Use the tapestry needle to punch holes about ½ inch (1.3 cm) apart around the edge of the coasters.

2. Cut off a piece of copper wire that is long enough to go around the edges of the coaster plus half of that length.

3. Beginning on the back side of one of the coasters, thread the wire through one of the holes, and pull it through until about an inch (2.5 cm) of wire is left on the back side.

4. Use the needle-nose pliers to twist the end of the wire and make

Simple coasters laced with wire and tiny beads make unusual breakfast companions.

a small spiral to keep the wire from pulling through the hole.

5. Thread five to nine seed beads onto the wire, and pull the wire to the back of the coaster before threading it up through the next hole. Continue to add beads, and whipstitch the edges of the coaster in this fashion.

6. After you've stitched through all of the holes, pull the end of the wire over the edge of the coaster and wrap it around the spiraled wire that you created in step 4.

7. Trim off the excess wire.

kitchen GOURD

Designer: VIRGINIA SAUNDERS

Spice up your kitchen with this delightful beaded container made from a cut and cleaned gourd. This is a simple project to try if you've never worked with wire and beads.

materials & tools

Purchased dried gourd (available at craft and hobby stores)

Pencil

Sharp knife

Small motorized cutting tool or small handheld power jigsaw

Grapefruit spoon

Metal scouring pad or coarse sandpaper

Fine-grit sandpaper

Mild detergent

Steel wool

Rubber gloves

Foam applicator brush

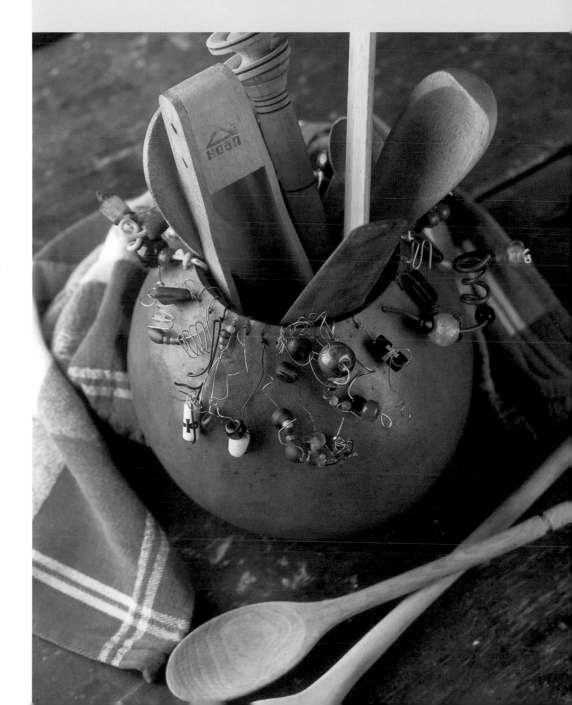

instructions

materials & tools, continued

Buckskin and medium brown leather dyes (may be purchased at leather supply outlets, craft stores, and shoe repair shops)

Damp sponge or towel

Polyurethane spray

Small handheld drill and $\frac{3}{32}$-inch (2.4 m) drill bit

Several types and sizes of wire of your choice (copper, steel, nylon-coated in colors)

Wire cutters

Round-nose pliers

A variety of brightly colored large beads

Small crochet hook, knitting needle, or chopstick

1. Use a pencil to mark a line around the circumference of the gourd where you'd like the edge of the utensil holder to fall. Make a slit along this line with the sharp knife.

2. Insert the cutting tool or jigsaw into the slit, and slowly cut around the line.

3. Take off the top of the gourd, and remove any seeds from the inside of the gourd with the grapefruit spoon. Once the gourd is clean, use the metal scouring pad or coarse sandpaper to smooth the inside walls. Sand again with the fine-grit sandpaper for a smooth, luscious interior.

4. Fill a sink with warm water and detergent, and gently wash the surface of the gourd. Use the steel wool to very gently (without scratching) remove spots from the surface.

5. After the gourd is cleaned and completely dry, put on the pair of rubber gloves to protect your hands. Use a foam brush to apply the two leather dyes to the surface to create a mottled effect. Allow the dye to soak into the surface and dry.

6. After the dye dries, wipe off the excess with a damp sponge or towel.

7. Protect the surface by spraying it with polyurethane. Allow the gourd to dry.

8. Mark dots around the edge of the top of the gourd that are about $\frac{1}{4}$ inch (6 mm) down from the top and $\frac{1}{2}$ inch (1.3 cm) apart.

9. Drill the holes with the handheld drill and bit.

10. Cut various small lengths of wire with the wire cutters, and pull pieces of wire through the holes to the front of the gourd. Secure the wires on the back with small curls made with the round-nose pliers.

11. Add beads randomly to the wires, and bend the ends around a crochet hook, knitting needle, or chopstick to create curlicues of different lengths and widths.

SALAD SERVING SET
with lampwork beads

Designer: SUSAN RIND

You don't need a special occasion to use these fabulous but functional servers.

materials & tools

Wire cutters

20-gauge stainless-steel wire, 3 yards (2.7 m)

Salad server set, silver or stainless steel with acrylic handles (ridged, if possible)

Needle-nose pliers

Round-nose pliers

125 or more assorted fire-polished faceted beads (8 mm)

10 or more flat oval lampwork beads

16 or more assorted fire-polished faceted beads (4 mm)

instructions

1. Cut two pieces of 16-inch-long (40.6 cm) stainless-steel wire.

2. Reserving a tail of about 3 inches (7.6 cm), wrap each of the wires twice in the groove of one of the utensil handles where the silver or stainless steel joins.

3. Use needle-nose pliers to twist the wire together where it joins. Randomly loop the wire with round-nose pliers to incorporate the short end and hide the twist.

4. Feed a couple of 8 mm beads onto the wire, followed by a flat oval bead. Alternate an 8 mm and a flat oval bead until the strand is the length of the handle. Clip the end of the wire, leaving a tail of a couple of inches (5.1 cm). Curl the wire end in small loops with the round-nose pliers to hold the beads on the strand in place.

5. Cut 10 pieces of wire, each 8 inches (20.3 cm) long.

6. Feed about ten 8 mm and two 4 mm beads on one of the wires to create a strand long enough to fit around the handle in the recess of the first ridge or ½ inch (1.3 cm) beneath the secured wire.

7. Wrap the strand around the acrylic handle, pulling both of the free ends of the wire to the top of the handle. Twist the unbeaded wire ends together so that the strand of flat beads made in step 4 is fastened down under the wire.

8. Use the round-nose pliers to loop and curl the excess wire in a random style to disguise the tightening join and ends.

9. Keep adding short strands of beads (as described in steps 6 through 8) until the handle is covered.

10. Repeat all of these steps to add beads and wire to the second serving piece.

(Note: After use, carefully hand wash the set in mild detergent before drying them with a clean cotton cloth.)

grapevine
NAPKIN RINGS

Designer: JANE DAVIS

materials & tools

For each napkin ring:

Wire cutters

1 yard plus 2 feet (1.5 m) of 18-gauge green wire

Round-nose pliers

26 inches (66 cm) of 26-gauge green wire

Wire jig (a board with pegs available at beading stores and some craft stores)

3 leaf beads, with two holes going through each bead

Small crochet hook, round chopstick, or other stick that is ⅛ inch (3 mm) in diameter or smaller

11 purple drop beads

Wire is braided and twisted to make these engaging, beaded napkin rings.

instructions

1. Cut three 20-inch (50.8 cm) lengths of 18-gauge green wire. Fold them in half, and pinch each fold tightly with the pliers.

2. Cut one 6-inch (15.2 cm) length of 26-gauge green wire, and string it through each of the three folded pieces of wire. (Set aside the rest of the wire for later.) Twist the ends of the 26-gauge wire together tightly. You now have three pairs of wire secured at the folds, ready to braid. Treat each doubled wire as one—lay them flat beside each other and avoid twisting them around one another as you work.

3. Place two pegs in the wire jig about ⅜-inch (9.5 mm) apart and spread your three wire pairs so that they straddle the pegs (figure 1).

4. To begin braiding the wires, bend the left wire pair over the middle wire pair (figure 2). Bend the right wire pair over the left wire pair, and pull the middle wire pair to the left. Place two new pegs about ⅜-inch (9.5 mm) below the first two pegs, so that the three wire pairs straddle the pegs again (figure 3).

5. Repeat step 4, adding new pegs until you run out of pegs or reach one end of the peg board. Remove all the pegs except the first six, and lift the wire off the pegs and reposition it so that you are ready to make the next braid in the wires. Continue working until your braid is about 5 inches (12.7 cm) long. Remove the braid from the peg board.

6. Twist two of the 18-gauge wire pairs around each other to secure the braid. Trim off the excess wire.

7. Bend the braid into a circle. Use the third 18-gauge wire pair (uncut) to close the circle by wrapping it around the start of the braid. Cut any excess wire close the wirework. (Leave the 26-gauge wire uncut, it will be used to secure the grapevine cluster to the braidwork.)

8. To make the tendril at the end of a leaf, fold the remaining 20 inches (50.8 cm) of the 26-gauge wire 5 inches (12.7 cm) from one end. Using the round-nose pliers,

Figure 1

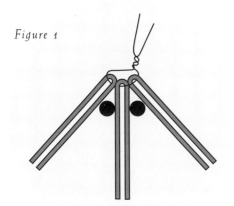

Figure 2

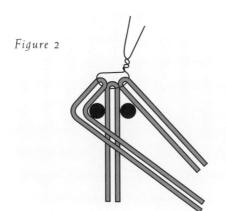

Figure 3

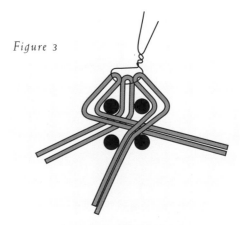

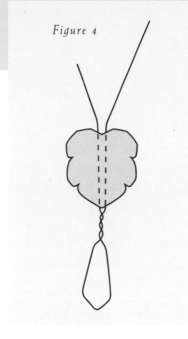

Figure 4

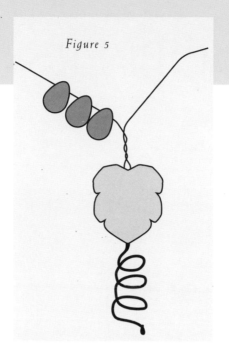

Figure 5

Figure 6

grab the folded wire about 2 inches (5.1 cm) from the fold. With your other hand, pinch the fold and twist it until you have a single, tightly wrapped strand of wire with a small loop at the end. Thread each end of the wire through the holes in the leaf bead from tip to base (figure 4).

9. Wind the 2 inches (5.1 cm) of twisted wire into a coil around the crochet hook. Remove the hook, and pull the tendril gently to give it a natural look. Twist the ends of the wire above the leaf together a few times to keep the leaf bead in place (figure 5).

10. To make the first grape cluster, thread three purple drop beads onto the shorter length of wire

above the leaf. Hold the beads together, and twist them around so the wires are twisted together above them (figure 6). Repeat this process with five purple beads on the longer length of wire.

11. Twist both wires together, then add another leaf on the long wire end, passing the wire up through the base toward the tip of the leaf. Leave a 2-inch (5.1 cm) loop of wire at the tip of the leaf. Twist this loop into a tendril as you did in step 8. Push the wire back through the other hole in the leaf, and twist it together with the other wire to hold the leaf in place.

12. Make three more grape clusters, and add one more leaf bead.

13. Attach the grape cluster to the napkin ring by winding the wire ends of it around the braidwork where the ends of the braid are joined together. Wind the wire ends from the braid around the cluster, then around the braid.

14. Arrange the leaves and grapes to cover the ends of the braid. Cut any excess wire close to the work, and bend the ends into the center so they won't catch on anything.

beautiful
BOTTLE TOPPERS

Crown a bottle filled with your favorite apertif with a festive

stopper embellished with wire and beads.

CONFETTI CORK

A wooden drawer pull is the base

for a riotous mix of colorful beads.

materials & tools

1¾-inch (4.4 cm) square wooden cabinet drawer pull

Paintbrush

Metallic paint (we used turquoise, orange, yellow, and lime)

Electric drill with ¹⁄₁₆-inch (1.6 mm) drill bit

Tapered bottle cork

White wood glue

Stainless-steel screw slightly longer than the length of your cork

Screwdriver

Designer: SUSAN RIND

Tube of fast-drying bead glue
or cement

1-inch (2.5 cm) flat glass bead

12 mm glass bead

20-gauge stainless-steel wire,
40-inch-long (1 m) piece

Faceted beads in
assorted colors

Round-nose pliers

instructions

1. Paint the drawer pull with swirls of metallic paint of various colors, and allow it to dry for a minimum of two hours.

2. Drill a ¹⁄₁₆-inch (1.6 mm) hole in each of the four corners of the cabinet drawer pull.

3. Center the pull on top of the bottle cork, and glue the cork to the pull with a bit of white wood glue. Allow the glue to set.

4. Drill up through the bottom of the cork and through the base of the finial. Use the screwdriver to screw the stainless steel screw through the hole that you drilled so that the cork is secured.

5. Use bead glue or cement to glue the flat bead to the top of the pull, followed by the 12 mm glass bead. Allow the stopper to dry for a minimum of 12 hours.

6. Wrap one end of the stainless-steel wire around the join between the cork and the pull, leaving a tail of 2½ inches (6.4 cm) free. Twist the tail around the rest of the wire twice to tighten and hold it in place.

7. Load the long end of the wire with assorted faceted beads, and wrap the wire and beads around the circumference of the base of the pull.

8. Twist the short, free end of the wire around the longer wire. Twist the wire around itself to secure the beads to the base. Thread the wire through the nearest drilled corner hole.

9. Moving around the drawer pull, loop the wire randomly with the round-nose pliers, adding beads as you go. When you arrive at a drilled corner, thread the wire down through a hole and back up to create a loop on the bottom side to add security to the piece. Each hole should have a few free-form wire loops over them to disguise them.

10. Secure the remaining wire around the flat bead and then around the top round bead, disguising the end in the free-form loops.

GLAMOUR STOPPER

This elegant stopper makes the most of the sensuous curves of a wooden finial.

materials & tools

3-inch-tall (7.6 cm) wooden finial

Metallic paints (we used blue, gold, and bronze)

Paintbrush

Tapered wine cork

Wood glue

Electric drill with ¹⁄₁₆-inch (1.6 mm) drill bit

Stainless-steel screw slightly longer than the cork

Screwdriver

20-gauge stainless-steel wire, 40-inch-long (1 m) piece

Round-nose pliers

Faceted beads in assorted colors

22-gauge copper wire, 5-foot-long (4.5 m) piece

instructions

1. Paint the finial with swirls of metallic paint, and allow it to dry for a minimum of two hours.

2. Center the finial on top of the cork, and glue the cork to it with white wood glue. Allow the glue to set.

3. Drill up through the bottom of the cork and through the base of the finial. Use the screwdriver to screw the stainless-steel screw through the hole that you drilled so that the cork is secured.

4. Wrap the stainless-steel wire twice around the join between the cork and the finial, leaving a short tail of about 3 inches (7.6 cm). Use the round-nose pliers to loop the wire in small curls around itself so that it is secured.

5. On the long wire remaining, thread on enough faceted beads to wrap twice around the lower portion of the finial. After you wrap the beads, wrap the wire around the finial once more to hold the strands in place.

6. Proceed up the finial by looping the wire randomly with the pliers, adding a few beads here and there until you reach the top.

7. Add a row of beads at the top of the finial (as you did in step 5 at the bottom of the finial), and finish forming the rest of the wire into random loops, taking care to hide the end of the wire.

8. Wrap the copper wire around the base, and twist it to secure it. Continue to randomly loop the wire up and around the wooden finial, moving in and out of the wire and beads that are already in place. Wrap it around the top of the finial, then finish off it by shaping a decorative spiral that rests flat on the front of the finial. Hide the end of it behind the spiral.

DRAGONFLY CORK

Allow this pleasant creature to light on

top of your favorite bottle.

materials & tools

Round cabinet pull

Metallic paints (we used lime, gold, and bronze)

Wire cutters

20-gauge stainless-steel wire, 30-inch-long (75 cm) piece

Round-nose pliers

Faceted beads in assorted colors (8 mm)

Flat oval lampwork bead (15 mm)

6–10 iridescent seed beads

2 pony beads

1-inch-wide (2.5 cm) masking tape

Cyanoacrylate glue

Wooden cabinet pull

instructions

1. Paint the cabinet pull with swirls of metallic paint, and allow it to dry for a minimum of two hours.

2. Duplicate the third through the eighth items listed under Materials and Tools on page 84, and follow steps 3 and 4 on page 85 to attach the cork to the cabinet pull.

3. Cut off a 30-inch-long (75 cm) piece of stainless-steel wire for the dragonfly form.

4. Bend the wire in half to double it, and twist it together twice at the bend.

5. Feed three faceted beads onto the ends of the doubled wire to form a tail. Slide them down to the bend in the wire. Add the oval lampwork bead for the body.

6. Separate the doubled wire, and bend it back and forth to make four wings, each approximately 1-inch (2.5 cm) long. Twist the wires together in the center to secure the wings.

7. Bring the ends of the wire together to form a double strand. Add two pony beads and separate the wires again. Add two seed beads onto each end to form the antennae.

8. Bend the ends of the wire down along the sides of the dragonfly's body. Pull one of the wire ends up on top of the wings. Add three faceted beads, and loop the beaded wire on top of the twist in the wings to hide it.

9. Loop this piece of wire over the oval bead to the underside of the dragonfly. Secure both ends of the wire underneath, then gently bend the naked wires up and out of the way.

10. Apply glue to the top of the cabinet pull, and use masking tape to secure the dragonfly in place. Allow it to dry there for at least 24 hours.

11. Bend the naked wires down over the cabinet pull. Wrap them around the base of the pull twice, and twist them together tightly.

12. Feed 12 to 14 faceted beads and two to four seed beads on the longer end of the wire. Wrap this piece around the base of the pull to cover the naked wire.

13. Use the shorter end of the wire to twist around the beaded wire, securing it tightly to the pull. Make a few loops to cover the twist and trim the wire. Weave the remaining wire end up and around the dragonfly. Hide the end of the wire in the beads.

fancy CONDIMENT SERVERS

Designer: SUSAN RIND

Dress up any party with these small, ingeneous masterpieces of imagination and engineering.

materials & tools

Silver or stainless-steel condiment knife, fork, and spoon with acrylic handles

Electric drill and small drill bit

Scrap of flat wood

Wire cutters

20-gauge stainless-steel wire, 30-inch (76.2 cm) piece

Round-nose pliers

60–70 assorted faceted beads (8 mm)

instructions

1. Place the fork and spoon face-up on a work surface with a scrap of wood underneath them. Use the electric drill fitted with a bit to drill a hole from front to back about ½ inch (1.3 cm) from the top of the acrylic handle of each utensil. Drill holes about ½ inch (1.3 cm) from the bottom of each handle. Tilt the blade of the knife so that it is perpendicular to your work surface, and follow the direction of the knife's blade to drill holes in both the top and bottom of the handle.

2. Cut a 10-inch-long (25.4 cm) piece of stainless-steel wire for each serving utensil. Anchor the wire at the top of each by threading about 3 inches (7.6 cm) of one end through the top hole. Wrap the wire around twice where the handle meets the metal, and leave 2 inches (5.1 cm) free.

3. Use pliers to twist the wire together on the front of each utensil where it meets, and loop the wire randomly to incorporate the short end.

4. Feed four to six 8 mm faceted beads onto the longer piece of wire on each utensil, and loop the wires and the beads randomly with the help of pliers, moving down the face of the utensil about ½ inch (1.3 cm). Loop the next portion of the wire (unbeaded) around the back of the handle to secure it before bringing it back to the front.

5. Repeat step 4 until you traverse the handles of each utensil, periodically feeding beads and wrapping around the handles until reaching the bottom hole.

6. Thread the remaining wire through the bottom hole, and wrap it around the handle to hold it in place. Twist tightly around one of the beads, and clip off any excess wire.

(Note: After use, carefully hand wash the set in mild detergent before drying them with a clean cotton cloth.)

golden
KNIFE AND SPOON

Designer: SUSAN RINI

materials & tools

Wire cutters

20-gauge stainless-steel wire, 40-inch-long (1 m) piece

Condiment spoon (silver or stainless steel)

Pâté knife (silver or stainless steel)

Round-nose pliers

8 or more rectangular gold-lined faceted beads (10 mm)

9 or more rectangular gold-lined faceted beads (8 mm)

4-inch (10.2 cm) piece of flexible beading wire (optional)

Silver crimp bead (optional)

Wrap the handles of a small knife and spoon with wire and gold-lined beads for a lovely effect.

instructions

1. Cut the wire into two 20-inch (50.8 cm) pieces. (One for each serving utensil.)

2. At the top of the spoon, wrap the wire around twice, leaving a 2-inch (5.1 cm) tail. Twist the shorter end around the longer wire. Loop the wire randomly to incorporate the shorter end and disguise the twist.

3. Feed one 10 mm gold-lined faceted bead onto the long end of the wire. Loop the wire around the bead, and then around the handle to secure the bead to the top of the handle.

4. Continue to add 10 mm faceted beads to the handle in this way, looping the wire in a free-form design until you traverse the length of the handle.

5. After securing the last bead, wrap the remaining wire around the handle and double back with wire underneath all of the wraps on the back of the handle of the spoon until you reach the top. Hide the end in free-form loops.

6. Repeat steps 2 through 5 to add 8 mm rectangular gold-lined faceted beads to the handle of the knife.

7. If your knife has a loop at the end of it (as ours does), you can add a beaded tassel to it. To do this, loop the flexible beading wire onto the end of the knife, add several remaining beads to the doubled wire, and end with a crimp bead. Flatten the crimp bead with pliers, and trim the wire.

(Note: Since these utensils are decorated with gold-lined faceted beads, be careful when washing them. Do not immerse them in soap and water, or you might lose some of the color inside the beads. Instead, wash the functional part of each by swabbing it with soap and water before rinsing it.)

wrapped GLASSES AND CONFETTI PARTY PICKS

You'll feel compelled to have guests once you've created

some of these beautiful glasses and matching party picks.

Designer: SUSAN RIND

WRAPPED GLASSES

Show off beautiful,

geometric-shaped cane

beads on a crooked stem.

materials & tools

For each glass:

Wire cutters

20-gauge stainless-steel wire
(at least 5-feet [1.5 m] length)

Needle-nose pliers

Wine, champagne, or martini glass
with sculptured stem

Assorted 8 mm faceted beads, cane
glass beads, or other glass beads

Round-nose pliers

instructions

1. Cut off a piece of wire about 5 feet (1.5 m) long. Leaving a tail of about 4 inches (10.2 cm), wrap the wire around the base of the stem twice to anchor it. Twist the two ends of the wire around each other, and tighten the wire with the aid of the needle-nose pliers.

2. To embellish a glass with 8 mm facetcd beads (such as you see on the standing glass in the background of the photo), use the same process outlined in the project on pages 95–96 (omitting the musical charm)—adding circular bands/ rows of beads around the top and bottom of the stem to fit the configuration of your stem.

3. To embellish a glass with cane glass beads or other larger beads (such as you see on the glass in the foreground), feed the beads randomly onto several inches of the longer wire before circling the bottom of the stem with the strand. Use pliers to curl and loop the shorter wire from step 1 on top of and through the circle of beads to anchor them. Hide the end of the short wire behind the strand.

4. Wrap the longer wire around the handle in the middle, moving upward as you go (leave this space free of beads for holding the glass).

5. Feed more cane beads onto the wire to fit the top of the stem, and secure them with wire loops as you did in step 3.

6. Hide the end of the wire behind the beads that are in place.

CONFETTI PARTY PICKS

Liven up any gathering with these

colorful beaded picks.

materials & tools

For each pick:

20-gauge stainless-steel wire

Locking pliers

Electric drill with bit removed

Coarse sandpaper

2 cane glass beads (10 to 12 mm)

6–8 assorted faceted beads (8 mm)

Needle-nose pliers

Flat-nose pliers

instructions

1. Cut off a 13-inch (33 cm) piece of the stainless-steel wire. Bend the wire in half.

2. Place an inch (2.5 cm) of the doubled wire (opposite the folded end) into the locking pliers and tighten them.

3. Place the folded end into the jaws of the drill (where the drill bit is normally placed), and tighten the drill as if it is holding a drill bit.

4. Turn on the drill to twist the wire slowly until an even braid is formed. Remove the braided wire, and snip it off on the non-folded end into a 4½-inch-long (11.4 cm) piece.

5. Use the sandpaper to sand the cut end.

6. Slide the two cane glass beads along the braided wire shaft to the folded end.

7. Cut off a 10-inch (25.4 cm) piece of wire. Wrap the wire five times around the shaft of the braided piece beneath the lower-most bead.

8. Continue looping the wire randomly around the two beads and adding additional beads to create the head of the pick.

9. Hide the end of the wire in the beads.

noteworthy GLASSES AND MUSICAL PICKS

Designer: SUSAN RIND

Serve your guests a before-the-concert cocktail in these clever musical glasses with matching picks.

NOTEWORTHY GLASSES

You'll be charmed by how simple it is to decorate your own glasses.

materials & tools

For each glass:

20-gauge stainless-steel wire, 1 yard plus 2 feet (1.5 m)

Wine or martini glass with gold decorative bulb at top of stem

About 30 gold-lined faceted beads (8 mm)

Round-nose pliers

1 rectangular gold-lined bead (10 mm)

Gold-plated musical charm

instructions

1. Leaving a tail of approximately 4 inches (10.2 cm), wrap the wire twice around the base of the glass stem before twisting it over on itself.

2. Feed eight to ten gold-lined faceted beads onto the long end of the wire, and circle the base of the stem with the wire. With the 4-inch (10.2 cm) tail, make small circular loops all the way around on top of this strand of beads.

3. Spiral up the stem of the glass with the long wire until you reach the bottom of the gold bulb at the top of the stem. Wrap the wire beneath the bulb, and feed eight more gold-lined faceted beads onto the wire. Wrap them around the top of the stem.

4. Stretch the wire up over the bulb, and wrap it around the stem above the bulb before feeding on 12 to 14 more faceted beads. Wrap the beads around the stem. Make small circles of wire with the pliers to hold the beads in place (as you did in step 2).

5. To create a visual focal point, use the pliers to bend the remaining wire into several large circular loops on top of one another, and feed the rectangular gold-lined bead onto the last loop. Slide a hanging musical charm onto the final loop. Hide the remaining end of the wire underneath the beads and wire.

MUSICAL PARTY PICKS

Twist pieces of stainless-steel wire to form a pick that you can decorate with instruments of your choice.

materials & tools

For each pick:

Wire cutters

20-gauge stainless-steel wire, 24-inch-long (61 cm) piece

Locking pliers

Electric drill with bit removed

Coarse sandpaper

Gold-plated button in the shape of a musical instrument

Rectangular gold-lined bead (12 mm)

Flat-nose pliers

Needle-nose pliers

instructions

1. Cut off a 13-inch (33 cm) piece of the stainless-steel wire. Bend the wire in half.

2. Place an inch (2.5 cm) of the doubled wire (opposite the folded end) into locking pliers and tighten them.

3. Place the folded end into the jaws of the drill (where the drill bit is normally placed), and tighten the drill as if it is holding a drill bit.

4. Turn on the drill to twist the wire slowly until an even braid is formed. Remove the braided wire, and snip it off on the non-folded end into a 4½-inch-long (11.4 cm) piece.

5. Use the sandpaper to sand the cut end.

6. Slide the button followed by one rectangular gold-lined bead along the braided wire shaft to the folded end.

7. Take the remaining piece of wire, and wrap the end of it beneath the gold-lined bead several times.

8. Stretch and spiral the wire up and around the bead before threading it through the hole in the button. Use pliers to loop the wire randomly behind the button to create the head of the pick.

9. Hide the end of the wire in the beads.

beaded
BOTTLE PEOPLE

Designer: BARBARA EVANS

These playful beings are made from bead, wires, and bottles.

Follow the instructions for the lady in the hat on the left,

or make up your own variations.

materials & tools

For bottle with lady and flowers:

26-gauge colored wire in several colors of your choice

Wire cutters

Flower and leaf beads for the bouquet and for embellishing the top of the hat (approximately 8 of each)

Several seed beads (optional)

¼-inch (6 mm) dowel

Round-nose pliers

Several accent beads (such as flowers and leaves) for the hat

Large bead that fits on top of the bottle (for the head)

materials & tools, continued

Long, tapered bead that fits comfortably inside the bottle opening

1 small bead (8 mm)

Sliced agate bead (for the hat)

Variety of stone beads for arms

Glass bottle

1 yard (.9 m) of ribbon, ¼ inch (6 mm) wide

Craft glue

instructions

For bottle with lady and flowers:

1. To make the beaded flower bouquet, cut several 3-inch (7.6 cm) lengths of 26-gauge wire for holding flower and leaf beads.

2. Slide one of the flower beads onto the middle of one of the wires. Fold the wire in half and twist the ends together tightly to form the stem. Repeat this process to add more flowers and leaves to the stems. (If some of your beads have a hole through the center of the flower, string the bead onto the wire and string a single seed bead on so that it sits in the cup of the flower. Push the end of the wire back through the center of the flower, pull tight, and twist the ends of the wire together.) When you're finished, set the stems aside.

3. Cut five 9-inch (22.9 cm) lengths of the colored wire. Wrap each of the wires tightly next to each other around the ¼-inch (6 mm) dowel (figure 1). Set the wires aside.

4. Cut six 4-inch (10.2 cm) lengths of colored wire to embellish the hat. Curl four of the wires around the end of the round-nose pliers to make tight curls for the top of the hat. Leave two wires uncurled. Attach accent beads (such as leaves and flowers) to the ends of the uncurled wires. Hold the beads in place by wrapping the tail of each wire around itself a few times at the base of the bead. Set these wires aside.

5. Line up the bead that you plan to use for the head with the long tapered bead that will fit inside the neck of the bottle. Cut a piece of 26-gauge wire that is double the length of these two beads, plus 5 inches (12.7 cm).

6. Push the small 8 mm bead onto the wire in the center, and then fold the wire in half. (This bead will keep the wire from pulling through the long bead.) Push the folded end of the wire up through the neck and head

Figure 1

bead. Add the sliced agate hat bead last. Pull the wire up tight.

7. Open the wire into a "V" at the top of the hat, and slide the curled and accented wires from step 4 inside of the "V." Twist the wire tightly to secure the wires on the top of the hat. Push the ends of the wire down, and clip so that they don't show.

8. Cut off a 3-inch (7.6 cm) piece of the 26-gauge wire. Peel off the wires you curled on the dowel in step 3, and wrap the entire bundle around the center with the piece of wire you just cut. Leave short sections of wire on both sides.

9. Take the bundle, and wrap the two free wires around the wire that connects the head bead and hat bead. Wrap each end around that wire several times, and curl the ends. Arrange the hair around the head bead.

10. To make the arms, cut a 30-inch (76.2 cm) length of the 26-gauge wire, and fold it in half. Twist the wires together close to the fold, leaving a small open loop

at the end. Lay out the two sets of beads that you plan to make into arms.

11. String the first set of beads (for one arm) onto both wires, so that the "hand" bead sits next to the loop you just made. String the second arm onto the wire, beginning with the shoulder beads.

12. Separate the two sets of arm beads at the middle of the doubled wires. Pull the two sections of wire apart slightly with the pliers to make an opening large enough to slip over the neck of your bottle.

13. Slip the arm beads over the neck of the bottle, and slide them until they rest tightly against the bottle. Thread the free ends of the wire through the loop at the end of the first arm. Pull them together gently, leaving a small gap between the hands for adding the bouquet you made in step 2.

14. Gather the stems of the bouquet into a bunch, and place them in the gap between the hands. Wrap the bouquet tightly with the tail of the wires.

15. Curl the ends of the wires into loose spirals with the round-nose pliers. Trim any excess wire.

16. Wrap the narrow ribbon around the neck of the bottle several times to hide the wire. Glue down the overlapping end in the back.

mesh BOX WITH BEADS

Designer: TERRY TAYLOR

materials & tools

Mesh-topped box

Masking tape

Wire cutters

32-gauge wire

Needle-nose pliers

Seed beads in several different colors (size 11)

20 or less metal beads

A mesh-topped box found at a thrift store is dressed up with a small explosion of beads in the center.

instructions

1. On the lid, use masking tape to mark off an area in the center where you'd like to place a configuration of beads.

2. Cut off several 12-inch (30.5 cm) lengths of wire.

3. Pull the end of one of the lengths of wire up through the mesh, leaving a tail of about an inch (2.5 cm). Secure the tail (on the back of the lid) by curling the wire with the needle-nose pliers.

4. String the beads on the long end of the wire in alternating colors. When you have strung about 2 inches (5.1 cm) of beads, string one silver bead on the end. Skip over the silver beads, and push the wire back through all of the other beads to the back of the lid.

5. Pull the wire tight with the needle-nose pliers. Weave underneath the lid to a new starting place near the strand that you just placed.

6. Repeat step 4, trim the wire to an inch (2.5 cm) or less, and secure the wire on the back of the lid, making a curl with the pliers.

7. Repeat this process to add as many strands of protruding beads as you want to the center area of the lid.

inspire

Cherish your life through reflective words in a beaded journal, pictures of loved ones in a jeweled frame, or dried flowers in sachets adorned with tiny beads.

JOURNAL *with beaded fringe*

Designer: LYNN B. KRUCKE

materials & tools

Purchased journal with Japanese stab binding (ours has four holes)

Measuring tape

Assorted fancy fibers, yarns, and metallic threads

Thin beading cord

Big-eye needle

Beads of many shapes and colors (with holes large enough to fit on the needle)

Seed beads (size 6)

Fast-drying bead glue

A cascading fringe laden with a treasure of beads transforms an empty journal into a book primed for your intimate thoughts.

instructions

1. Remove the binding ribbon from the journal, and make notes on how the ribbon is threaded so that you can rethread it in the same way later.

2. Measure the length of the ribbon that you remove from the journal, and cut the fancy fibers, yarn, metallic thread, and beading cord into pieces long enough to rethread the binding and make a tail that hangs down the front of the journal.

3. Gather all of the pieces into a bundle, and rethread the holes in the journal, tying off the bundle on the front.

4. Begin stringing the larger beads onto the various fibers in the bundle with the big-eye needle. (To do this, thread the needle onto the end of a fiber, and string on the assorted beads.)

5. Cover some of the beading cord strands entirely with the seed beads and an occasional accent bead (you won't need a needle to string beads on the beading cord). When you have reached the desired length, tie a knot in the bottom of the thread to keep the beads from sliding off. Dab some glue onto the knot.

6. To "float" some of the beads, string on a few beads, tie a knot underneath them, and then tie a knot where you want your next line of beads to begin on the thread or cord (figure 1). String on more beads, and tie off at the end of this line of beads. Make as many beaded sections in the cord as you want.

7. String beads until you like the way your beaded fringe looks. Glue all of the knots and trim the fibers to an equal length.

Figure 1

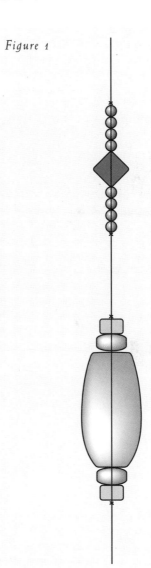

embossed & beaded
FRAME

Designer: BRENDA L. SPITZER

materials & tools

Large, flat paintbrush

10-inch (25.4 cm) square wooden frame with 3½-inch (8.9 cm) square opening (a board cut into this size will work also)

Dark blue acrylic paint

Metal picture hanger

8 clear glass cabochons (flat glass marbles)

White vinegar

Paper towels

Glass paints in white, yellow, orange, red, light blue, dark blue, and green

Small round paintbrush

Clear medium made for glass painting

Heavy scissors suitable for cutting metal

A simple metal embossing technique and painted cabachons are paired to make a frame that is an art object in itself.

9 ¼ x 12-inch (23.5 x 30.5 cm) piece of medium aluminum embossing metal

Computer mouse pad

Masking tape

Photocopy of embossing template (see page 106)

Stylus for metal embossing

Craft knife

Spackling compound

Putty knife

Acrylic matte spray sealer

Light ivory acrylic paint

Clear acrylic glaze

Small sea sponge

8 upholstery tacks, ⅜-inch (9.5 mm) diameter

Hammer

Craft adhesive suitable for glass and metal

32 large cane glass beads

16 blue seed beads (size 5)

16 red seed beads (size 5)

32 green seed beads (size 5)

32 yellow seed beads (size 5)

instructions

1. Use the large, flat paintbrush to coat the wooden frame on all sides with dark blue acrylic paint. Set it aside to dry. Attach the metal picture hanger to the back of the frame.

2. To create the "millefiore" beads, rinse the cabochons in a mixture of white vinegar and water. Dry them off thoroughly with paper towels.

3. Using the glass paints and the small round paintbrush, begin painting on the flat side of each of the eight beads. Refer to figure 1 (next page) for ideas on the sequence of painting shapes to create flowers. (Keep in mind that whatever you paint on first will end up on top of your image, so you'll work from the center of the flower out to the petals.) Allow each layer of paint to dry before adding the next layer.

4. After all the layers of paint dry, apply a coat of the clear medium. Set the beads aside to dry.

5. Use heavy scissors to cut the embossing metal into a 9¼-inch (23.5 cm) square, and place it on top of the mouse pad.

6. Tape the photocopy of the embossing pattern to the metal square. To emboss the metal, use the pointed end of the stylus to trace the outline of the entire pattern. Make sure to keep the mouse pad under the areas that you're working on, since embossing over a soft surface allows for greater definition of the pattern.

7. Once the pattern has been traced, remove it and turn the embossed metal over on the mouse pad. (This side is the front of the frame.) To further define the pattern refer to figure 2 (next page), and trace around the pattern with the pointed end of the stylus where indicated (excluding the round centers). Use the rounded end of the stylus to emboss each of the round centers in the squares.

8. Turn the embossed metal over again, so that the back side is facing up, and refer to figure 3 (next page). To make the four petals in each square stand out, use the rounded end of the stylus to emboss the petals as indicated in the diagram.

9. Use the craft knife to cut out the center of the embossed metal for the opening in the frame.

10. On the back of the embossed metal square, fill in the embossed petals with the spackling compound and putty knife. Allow the compound to dry.

Figure 1

Figure 2

Figure 3

11. Spray the front of the embossed metal square with acrylic matte sealer, and allow it to dry.

12. Mix one part light ivory acrylic paint to one part clear glaze to one part water. Using the sea sponge, lightly sponge the mixture over the front of the embossed metal and over the heads of the eight upholstery tacks. Allow the metal and nails to dry.

13. Center the embossed metal square over the front of the wooden frame. Use the upholstery tacks to fix the metal to the wooden frame at the outer and inner corners.

14. Use the finished piece as a guide to positioning and gluing the cabachons and colored beads to the metal.

Embossing template: enlarge 155%

bead and wire
CD CLOCK

Designer: LYNN B. KRUCKE

Salvage a CD destined for the trash, and make it into a clever, decorative timepiece.

materials & tools

Sea sponge

Acrylic paints in colors of your choice (we used pearl emerald, pearl turquoise, and pearl blue)

Junk CD

Pencil

Double-sided adhesive sheet

Sheet of cardstock in color of your choice

Craft knife

Scrap paper

Small handheld drill

Set of number stamps

Permanent black ink

22-gauge wire in color of your choice (we used teal)

Ruler

Wire cutters

Round-nose pliers or wooden skewer

Assortment of beads of your choice

Clockworks for ¼-inch-thick (6 mm) clock face

Strong craft glue

Item(s) to cover center of clock, such as a selection of beads to glue around the shaft of the clockworks, a fender washer (a large washer available at home and hardware stores), or a small, thin doughnut-shaped bead

instructions

1. Apply acrylic paints to the shiny side of the CD with the damp sea sponge until you like the look of the surface. Allow the paints to dry completely.

2. Trace the outline of the CD onto a sheet of double-sided adhesive as well as the sheet of card stock, and cut out the circles. Adhere one side of the adhesive sheet to the unpainted (reverse) side of the CD, and stick the cardstock circle to the other side.

3. Use the craft knife to carefully remove the excess cardstock from the center hole in the CD.

4. Trace the CD onto a piece of scrap paper, and cut it out. Fold the paper in half, and then in quarters. Crease the folds well, and unfold them. Use this template to mark the 12, 3, 6, and 9 positions around the face of the CD, about ¼ inch (6 mm) from the edge.

5. Use the small drill to carefully drill holes in the CD at the points that you marked.

6. Using the finished piece as a guide, stamp numbers with permanent black ink around the face of the clock.

7. Measure out and cut two 8-inch (20.3 cm) lengths and two 3-inch (7.6 cm) lengths of wire.

8. Starting at one end of a shorter wire, use the tips of the round-nose pliers or a skewer to wrap the wire and make a small loop. Continue wrapping the wire around by hand to create a tight spiral. After several wraps, bend the remaining wire so that it is perpendicular to the spiral. Thread the straight end of the wire through the 12 o'clock hole from back to front so that the spiral rests flat on the back side of the CD and secures the wire.

9. From the front side of the CD, place a bead on the wire. Trim the remaining exposed wire to approximately 1½ inches (3.8 cm), then wrap it around pliers or a skewer and curl it until it fits tightly on top of the bead. Repeat this process with wire and a bead at the six o'clock position.

10. Bring one of the longer lengths of wire through the hole at the three o'clock position until you have equal parts of wire protruding in the front and back. Bring both ends of the wire together at the edge of the CD, twisting them together tightly to secure them. Add beads on each wire and twist the excess wire to secure them. Shape the wire and beads to fit the clock face as you wish. Repeat this process with wire and beads at the nine o'clock position.

11. Use strong glue to attach the clockworks on the back of the CD, making sure that the notch for hanging is at the top. Install the hands for the clock as directed by the manufacturer, and glue extra beads, a fender washer, or doughnut-shaped bead in place to conceal the opening and the clock mechanism.

bugle bead
VASE DRAPE

Designer: LINDA KALWEIT

Though impressive, this drape made of four bead ladders is simple to master. Drape it onto your favorite vase or decanter, and it'll brighten a table or mantle in your home.

materials & tools

Size 12 beading needle

Nylon beading thread that matches the bugle beads

20 mm bugle beads (160 pieces or 40 grams)

Accent beads: 60 grams of cubes (4 x 4 mm), triangles (size 5), and faceted beads (4 mm)

Nail polish with nylon (non-acetone)

Scissors

Bowl

Measuring tape

Vase or bottle (the neck must be smaller than the base)

instructions

1. To make the bugle bead ladders (the rectangular drapes that hang down the sides of the bottle), thread your beading needle and string on two bugle beads. Leave a 6-inch (15.2 cm) tail (figure 1).

2. Pass back through the first bugle you strung, entering the side of the bead where the tail is sticking out. Pull it tight so the beads stack next to each other (figure 2).

3. Pass through the second bugle bead (figure 3), and string on another bugle bead. Go back through the second bugle bead, so that the one you just added stacks against it (figure 4).

4. Repeat until you have a ladder that is a good length for your vase.

5. String on several accent beads to make a loop that dangles off the bottom of the bugle bead ladder. Sew through the final bugle bead and the loop several times for strength (figure 5).

6. Sew up through several rows of bugles in the ladder. Brush about an inch (2.5 cm) of your thread with nail polish, and sew into several more bugle beads. Cut the thread close to the ladder.

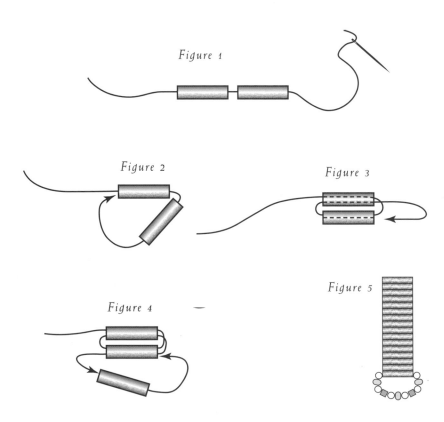

Figure 1

Figure 2

Figure 3

Figure 4

Figure 5

7. Repeat steps 1 through 6 to make three more ladders.

8. Lay the ladders in a circle, leaving spaces between them to add strands of accent beads. Mix all of your accent beads in a bowl.

9. Measure the neck of your bottle and add ½ inch (1.3 cm) to this measurement. Jot down this figure. Multiply the length of one of your bugle beads by four, subtract this measurement from the figure you wrote down, and divide the resulting figure by four. This measurement will tell you the length of each row of beads that you should add on the first row between the ladder.

10. Thread your needle and double the thread. Tie a knot in the end. Sew through the top bugle in the first ladder, add beads to create the length that you figured, and sew through the second ladder. Continue until all four ladders are connected. (They should be evenly spaced and fit around the neck of your bottle with ½ inch [1.3 cm] to spare.)

11. Sew through the entire circle one more time for additional strength.

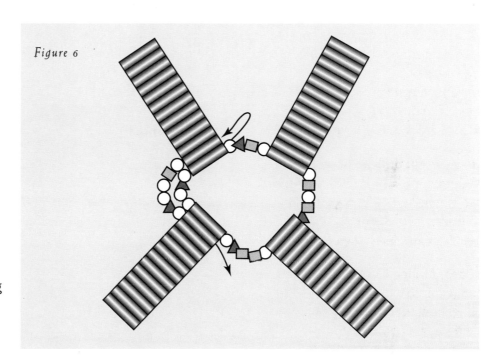

Figure 6

12. Go through the bugle bead immediately below the one you are exiting, and push the needle through in the opposite direction. Continue to add beads between the ladders until you complete the circle (figure 6). (You'll add a few more beads between each ladder to make the drape.)

13. After adding this second round of beads, thread the needle back and forth through the next two

bugle beads (so that you skip a bead before adding another drape). String on another row of beads—adding more beads to make the drape longer.

14. When you are satisfied with the drape you've created, sew back through the bugle beads, and brush nail polish onto the end of your thread. Pass through a few more beads, and closely trim your thread.

HANGING BASKET
with glass beads

materials & tools

14-gauge galvanized wire

Wire cutters

Round-nose pliers

12–15 large glass beads with holes

The interesting visual rhythms of this functional wire basket are courted by a fringe of large hanging beads.

Designer: TERRY TAYLOR

instructions

1. Cut the wire into 5-inch (12.7 cm) lengths, one for each bead you plan to hang on the basket.

2. Use the pliers to make a C-shaped loop at the top of each piece of wire.

3. Place a bead on the other end of each wire.

4. Use the pliers to make a loop below each bead to hold it in place.

5. Hang the beaded wires along the rim and on the bottom of the basket. As you go, close each of the C-shaped loops so that the wire stays in place on the basket.

spiral design SACHET

Designer: CINDY GORDER

Whether on display in your boudoir, or tucked away in a private drawer, this sachet will provide you with a sensual reprieve.

materials & tools

Photocopy of template (page 114)

Scissors

7 x 8-inch (17.8 x 20.3 cm) piece of silk fabric

7 x 8-inch (17.8 x 20.3 cm) piece of fusible interfacing

Iron

Erasable fabric marker

Metallic embroidery braid, fine or very fine

Embroidery needle

Nylon beading thread

Size 12 beading needle or appliqué needle

Seed beads that complement fabric (size 11)

7 x 12-inch (17.8 x 30.5 cm) piece of organza or other sheer fabric

Sewing machine and thread

Seed beads in 3 different colors (size 8)

Triangular seed beads (size 8)

½ cup (112 grams) of lavendar seeds

Sewing thread and needle

instructions

1. Cut out the front template, place it on the piece of silk fabric, and cut out the shape. Cut the same shape from the fusible interfacing, and trim off about ¼ inch (6 mm) around the outside edge. Fuse the interfacing to the wrong side of the fabric.

2. Use the template as a guide to draw the double spiral pattern onto the right side of the silk with the erasable fabric marker.

3. Thread the embroidery needle with the fine metallic braid, and work the spiral pattern with a blanket stitch (see page 117).

4. Use the beading thread and needle to stitch a single size 11 seed bead to the silk along the top of each point of the blanket stitches (see finished photo).

5. Use the other two patterns to cut out two pieces of organza or other sheer fabric for the backing.

Template for front of pillow

Enlarge 200%

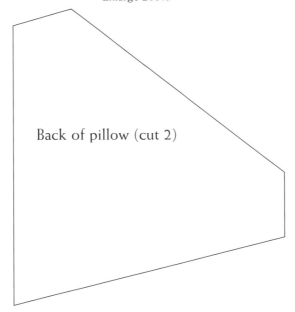

Back of pillow (cut 2)

6. Press down the center edges of the backing pieces. With right sides together, and the backing pieces overlapping in the middle to fit the front piece, stitch the front and back together. Trim the corners and turn right side out.

7. Thread the beading needle with beading thread, and knot the end. Anchor a stitch at one of the diamond's points.

8. Pick up a size 8 seed bead, five size 11 seed beads, one triangular seed bead, and one size 11 seed bead. Skip the last bead and go back up through the triangle. Continue through all the beads to the top of the fringe. Take a ¼-inch (6 mm) stitch, and add another strand. Continue to add strands until you've covered the outside edge of the sachet.

9. Fill the sachet with lavender, and secure the back by whipstitching the seam by hand.

crazy QUILT PILLOW

Designer: CINDY GORDER

materials & tools

Photocopies (both black and white and color) of family photos or printed papers

Transfer medium

White cotton fabric

Scissors

Erasable fabric marker

13 x 17-inch (33 x 43.2 cm) piece of cotton batting (or 1 inch [2.5 cm] larger than the pillow form)

Iron

Fusible interfacing

Scraps of colored fabric of your choice

Sewing needle and thread for basting

Embroidery threads in colors of your choice

Embroidery and chenille needle

Small bits of fabric and nostalgic photos are framed with beads and embroidery to make an heirloom pillow.

Straight pins

Fine metallic cord or thread

Seed and bugle beads of various sizes and colors

Size 12 beading needle or appliqué needle

Nylon beading thread

Fancy trims

Fancy beads and charms

Ribbon flowers

1½-inch-wide (3.8 cm) ribbon, 7 feet (2.1 m) long

13 x 22-inch (33 x 55.9 cm) piece of fabric for the back (or piece that is 1 inch [2.5 cm] wider and 6 inches [15.2 cm] longer than the pillow)

Sewing machine and thread

12 x 16-inch (30.5 x 40.6 cm) pillow form, or size of your choice

instructions

1. Choose personal family photos and/or printed materials (such as wedding invitations, graduation announcements, etc.) that you'd like to use as components on your pillow top.

2. Follow the manufacturer's instructions on the transfer medium to transfer the photos and printed materials to the cotton fabric. Cut out the transfers, leaving a ½-inch (1.3 cm) border of fabric around each image.

3. Use the fabric marker to mark a ½-inch (1.3 cm) seam allowance on all sides of the cotton batting (your pillow foundation). Put the foundation piece aside.

4. To make a stitched letter patch for your pillow top (see the lower right-hand side of our pillow for an example), iron fusible interfacing to the back of a silky fabric or other fabric of your choice for reinforcement. Draw script or letters on the patch with the erasable fabric marker. Stitch the design with embroidery thread using a stem stitch (see page 117).

5. Beginning with the transfer and stitched letter patches as a focus for your design, arrange scraps of fabric around them on top of the pillow foundation, allowing ½-inch (1.3 cm) seam allowance on the pieces.

6. Pin and baste the patches into place on the pillow foundation, overlapping them ¼ to ½ inch (6 mm to 1.3 cm). Fold the raw edges of the top patches under ¼ to ½ inch (6 mm to 1.3 cm).

7. Working from the outside in, use basic embroidery stitches (see page 117) sewn in embroidery threads and fine metallic cord or thread as well as trims to cover all the seams and hold the patchwork in place. Anchor all of your threads by taking several small straight stitches in the same spot before starting or ending a thread.

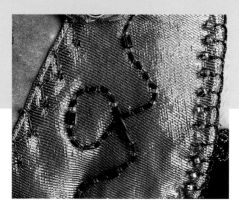

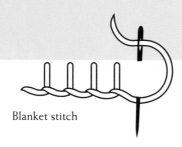

Blanket stitch

Sheaf filling

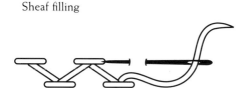

Chevron stitch

8. Add seed or bugle beads to the embroidered seams using the beading needle and thread. Tack down fancy trims with a similar color embroidery thread. Add the fancy beads, charms, and ribbon flowers wherever you want them.

9. Cut the 1½-inch-wide (3.8 cm) ribbon into 3-inch (7.6 cm) lengths. Fold each length in half. Turn the lengths at a 45° angle and pin them along the edge of the pillow front on the seam line, with the tips pointing toward the center front. Baste them in place along the seam line.

10. Cut the fabric for the back in half widthwise. Finish one of the short edges on each half with a narrow hem sewn on your machine. Overlap the hemmed edges at the center to conform to the pillow top (right sides up).

11. Place the pillow back right side down on the front of the pillow top, and pin the pieces together. Stitch around all four sides with a ½-inch (1.3 cm) seam allowance. Trim the corners and turn the pillow right side out. Insert the pillow form.

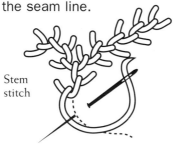

Stem stitch

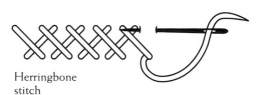

Herringbone stitch

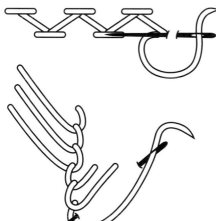

Maidenhair stitch

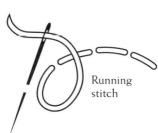

Running stitch

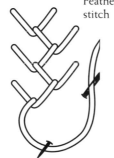

Feather stitch

Beaded ribbon (ribbon gathered and stitched down with beads)

lavender & rose SACHETS

Designer: NANCY WORRELL

These delicate sachets will make you nostalgic for times past.

RUFFLED LAVENDER SACHET

Sheer windowpane fabric is dotted with a pattern of small silver beads.

materials & tools

2 pieces of solid sheer fabric for ruffle, 2½ x 14 inches (6.4 x 35.6 cm) each

Windowpane checked sheer fabric, 3½ x 7 inches (8.9 x 17.8 cm)

Scissors

Sewing machine and thread

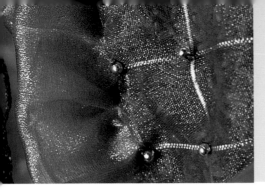

materials & tools, continued

Dried lavender

Size 12 beading needle or appliqué needle

Nylon beading thread

About 25 silver beads (3 mm) or other small beads of your choice

instructions

1. Fold the pieces of solid sheer fabric in half lengthwise and gather them along the raw edges. Draw up the gathers to make ruffles to fit the long sides of the checked fabric. Pin together the raw edges of both with the right sides facing. Stitch with a $\frac{1}{2}$-inch (1.3 cm) seam allowance.

2. Fold the piece in half lengthwise with right sides together so that the short edges are aligned. Sew up the long sides with a $\frac{5}{8}$-inch (1.6 cm) seam allowance, catching the ruffles as you go. Stitch the short edges together, leaving a small opening in the center for turning the pillow.

3. Turn the right side of the pillow out, positioning the seam in the center back. Spoon lavender seeds into the opening and then stitch it closed.

4. Sew silver beads to the corners of each square.

SQUARE SACHET

Use the lines in the pattern provided or make up one of your own to stitch on your favorite bugle and seed beads.

materials & tools

Piece of black netting

Embroidery hoop

Light-colored dressmaker's pencil

Black nylon beading thread

Size 12 beading needle or appliqué needle

Seed and bugle beads in a variety of colors

Scissors

Sewing machine and black thread

3-inch (7.6 cm) square piece of black fabric for backing

instructions

materials & tools, continued

Potpourri

Tapestry needle

Metallic ribbon thread

Figure 1

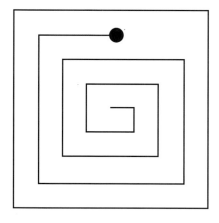

1. Secure the black netting in the embroidery hoop. Mark off a 2-inch (5.1 cm) square in the center of the net with the dress-maker's pencil.

2. Use the embroidery needle and thread to stitch seed and bugle beads in a pattern, using figure 1 as a guide. To do this, thread the needle with black thread, and tie a knot in the end of one thread. Pull the thread up through the net at the dot indicated on figure 1. String on one seed, one bugle, and anoth-er seed bead. Go back through the netting, and pull the thread tight. Come back up through the netting at the point adjacent to the last seed bead. Continue to add beads in this fashion to form a line of beads. Tie off the thread on the back, and remove the net from the hoop.

3. With the beaded square in the center, cut the netting into a 3-inch (7.6 cm) square. Place the right sides of the beaded square and the black fabric square together. Stitch them together with a narrow seam, leaving a small hole for turning the sachet.

4. Turn the sachet right side out, and fill it with potpourri. Stitch the hole closed.

5. Thread the tapestry needle with the ribbon thread and finish the edge of the sachet with a blanket stitch. Use additional thread to make a bow and loop for hanging.

SHADOW-QUILTED ROSE HEART SACHET

The subtle overlay of fabric in this sachet makes it especially lovely for holding rosebuds.

materials & tools

Scraps of sheer silver or white fabric

Light-colored dressmaker's pencils

Embroidery hoop

Size 12 beading needle or appliqué needle

White nylon beading thread

About 70 silver beads (3 mm)

Small dried rosebuds or rose petals

White embroidery thread and needle

Sewing machine

12 inches (30.5 cm) of white cord with silver pearls

12 inches (30.5 cm) of white ribbon, ⅛ inch (3 mm) wide

instructions

1. Draw a 3½-inch (8.9 cm) circle on the sheer fabric with the dressmaker's pencil. Draw a heart in the center of the circle.

2. Secure the fabric in the embroidery hoop, thread the needle with white beading thread, and stitch the silver beads with a running stitch around the heart's outline. Remove the fabric from the hoop.

3. Place a couple of small crushed rosebuds or rose petals on the front of the netting within the beaded heart. Cover this piece with another piece of sheer fabric, and stretch both taut in the hoop so that the heart and petals are covered by the second layer of fabric.

4. Use white embroidery thread to backstitch around the inside and outside edges of the beaded heart, securing the rose petals between the fabrics. Remove the fabrics from the hoop.

5. Cut the layered fabric into a 3½-inch (8.9 cm) circular piece, using the drawn circle from step 1 as a guide for cutting.

6. From another piece of sheer fabric, cut a 3½-inch (8.9 cm) circle to serve as the backing. Place the right sides together, and stitch with the machine around the circle leaving a small opening for turning. Turn to the right side. Fill the sachet with the remaining rosebuds, and stitch it closed.

7. Beginning at the top, above the heart, position the white cord with silver pearls along the seam. Hand stitch the cord to the circle.

8. Tie a piece of ribbon into a bow, and tack it to the top center of the sachet.

jeweled FRAMES

Designer: SUSAN RIND

Add wire and beads to the edges of readymade frames to show off your favorite subjects.

SIMPLE FLOWER FRAME

Create a simple wire flower to adorn a frame's edge.

materials & tools

1 mm silver-plate wire, 3 yards plus 3 inches (3.25 m)

Wire cutters

Round-nose pliers

25 assorted faceted beads (4 mm to 12 mm)

Cyanoacrylate glue

4 x 6-inch (10.2 x 15.2 cm) picture frame with a wide, metallic frame

instructions

1. Cut the silver-plate wire into three 29-inch (73.7 cm) lengths.

2. Hold all three wire strands together about 2 inches (5.1 cm) from the ends. Make a bend in each of the wires about 1½-inches (3.8 cm) above this point. Loop the wires back onto themselves, and twist them together once at the bottom to hold them in place. These three looped wires will become three petals.

3. Repeat step 2 four more times to add 12 more loops/petals. Loosely fan out the petals to form a flower shape as you go.

4. Choose one of the hanging strands of wire, and feed all of the faceted beads onto it in random order. Wind this loaded wire in circles in the center of the flower until it is full of beads.

5. With the remaining 29-inch (7.5 cm) wires, weave up and down, over and under beads to hold the beaded wires in place. To finish the loose ends, loop and curl the wire to create an interesting design on top of the flower. Hide the ends of the wire.

6. Use the round-nose pliers to open up the petals, separate, and bend them. Make a small kink at the top of each petal by crimping the wire gently with the pliers.

7. When you've finished forming the beaded flower, glue it to one corner of the frame. Allow it to dry for 24 hours.

EASY JEWELED FRAME

This elaborate-looking but simple-to-make frame is created with pieces of costume jewelry, wire, and beads.

materials & tools

Toothpicks

Cyanoacrylate glue

Old or new costume jewelry

Frame of your choice with at least a 2-inch (5.1 cm) width

Wire cutters

20-gauge stainless-steel wire

Needle-nose pliers

Round-nose pliers

Assorted faceted and metal beads (4 to 12 mm)

instructions

1. Use toothpicks to apply cyanoacrylate glue to the backs of the pieces of jewelry. Glue the jewelry around the edges of the frame. Allow the frame to dry for 24 hours.

2. Cut off four 20-inch (50.8 cm) lengths of the stainless-steel wire.

3. Use the needle-nose pliers to hold the wire, and the round-nose pliers to loop the wires in and out of the jewelry pieces, adding assorted beads and making small decorative circles as you go.

4. Hide the ends of the wires by tucking them underneath the jewelry pieces or loops of wire.

painted and embroidered
SILK PILLOW

Designer: CINDY GORDER

materials & tools

7 x 9½-inch (17.8 x 24.1 cm) panel of white silk

Wax paper

Blue, purple, and green fabric dyes

Paintbrushes

Iron

6 x 8½-inch (15.2 x 21.6 cm) rectangle of fusible interfacing

Embroidery needle

Fine metallic embroidery braid for front of pillow

Perle cotton embroidery thread (size 5) for front of pillow

Silk ribbon for front of pillow

Variety of beads for front of pillow (see figure 1, page 126)

2 pieces of silky fabric for backing, 7 x 6 inches (17.8 x 15.2 cm) each

Reserve a place of honor on your most respectable chair for this treasure of embroidery and beads.

Sewing machine and thread

Straight pins

Scissors

Size 12 beading needle or appliqué needle

Nylon beading thread

Medium bugle beads (½ inch [1.3 cm] long) for decorative border on seam

Seed beads in color of your choice for decorative border on seam and fringe (size 8)

Short bugle beads for fringe

Several different colors of seed beads for fringe (size 11)

Small dagger-shaped beads for fringe

4 mm cubes for fringe

Teardrop-shaped beads for fringe

Seed beads for fringe (size 6)

Polyester pillow stuffing

instructions

1. Place the silk panel on a sheet of wax paper. Paint streaks of fabric dye onto the silk. Overlap the dyes to create washes.

2. Allow the silk to dry, and then heat set it according to the manufacturer's instructions.

3. Center the fusible interfacing on the back of the pillow, and iron it into place following the manufacturer's instructions. (This backing will provide support for the beadwork.)

4. Refer to the stitch and bead chart (figure 1, next page) and the stitch guide (page 117) to embroider the pillow top with various stitches, beads, and ribbons. Keep all of your stitching and beadwork away from the ½-inch (1.3 cm) seam allowances.

5. Press a 1-inch (2.5 cm) fold on one of the short ends of each of the silky backing pieces. With the right sides up, overlap the pressed edges at the center to form a 7 x 9½ inch (17.8 x 24.1 cm) rectangle.

6. Place the right side of the pillow top on the backing pieces, and pin the pieces together. Stitch around all four sides with a ½-inch (1.3 cm) seam allowance. Trim the corners, and turn the pillow right side out.

7. Thread the beading needle with the beading thread. At the seam of the pillow, in an inconspicuous spot, take several small stitches on top of each other to anchor the thread.

8. Using a running stitch, alternate a ½-inch (1.3 cm) bugle bead with a size 8 seed beads around the entire pillow seam (figure 2, page 127). At the corners, adjust the number of seed beads in order to fit the line of beads around the curves. When you reach the place where you started, pass back through several beads, and exit from a seed bead.

9. Pick up three size 11 seed beads in one color, one size 8 seed bead, three size 11 seed beads in another color, three more size 11 seed beads in another color, one size 8 seed bead, one short bugle

bead, one size 8 seed bead, and a small dagger-shaped bead. Skip the dagger bead, and go back up through the last three beads you put on. String on a series of seed beads that matches the line of beads that are strung on the other side of the "V" (six size 11 seed beads, one size 8 seed bead, and three size 6 seed beads). Thread the needle through the next seed bead stitched to the seam (figure 3).

10. Pick up two size 11 seed beads, one size 6 seed bead, one cube, and one teardrop-shaped bead. Skip the final bead, and go back up through the beads to the top of the fringe. Go back through the same bead, entering from the left side, and back out again (figure 4).

11. Repeat the last two steps to add fringe around the perimeter of the pillow. At each corner, string a few larger beads close to the fabric, then add a few strands of random beads to form tassels.

12. To finish your pillow, fill it with polyester stuffing, and whipstich it closed at the center seam.

Figure 1

A   Button stitch with size 11 seed beads

B   Running stitch with 3 mm bugle beads

C   Running stitch with size 11 seed beads

D   Maidenhair stitch with size 11 seed beads

E   Beaded ribbon with size 8 seed beads

F   Running stitch with size 11 seed beads and accent leaf beads

G   Maidenhair stitch with size 11 seed beads

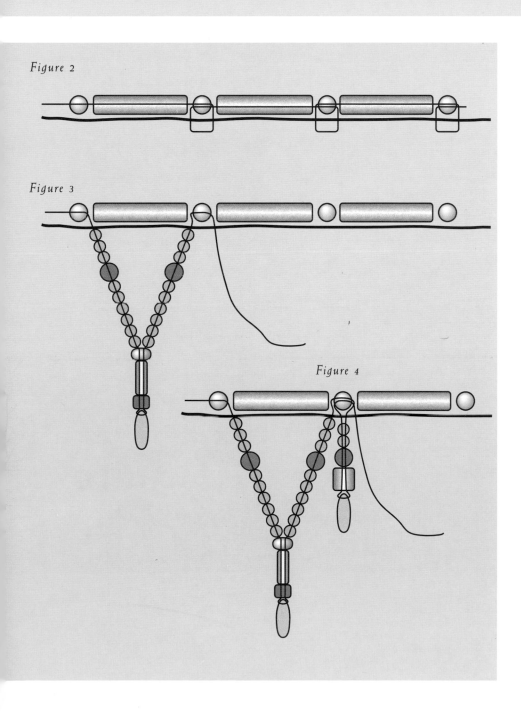

Figure 2

Figure 3

Figure 4

DESIGNERS

Sandie Abel (Madison, Wisconsin) has been a fiber artist for 30 years and participated in the creation of Judy Chicago's "Birth Project." She took up beadwork a few years ago, and enjoys working on innovative ideas in this medium.

Jane Davis (Ventura, California) is a designer who writes books and patterns about a variety of needle arts, from beadwork and quilting to crochet and knitting. She is the author of two forthcoming Lark Books on crochet and knitting with beads.

Barbara Evans (Ventura, California) is a nationally recognized dollmaker who creates dolls in a variety of media. Her work is published in craft magazines and books.

Cindy Gorder (Miineral Point, Wisconsin) has been a professional graphic artist for over 25 years. She has been involved with the craft industry for the past 14 years, and now designs craft projects for publication in a variety of media.

Heather Horne (Asheville, North Carolina) began experimenting with beads when she was pregnant with her second child. She now works full-time at Chevron Trading Post in Asheville, North Carolina.

Linda Kalweit (Duluth, Minnesota) is the owner of The Bead Palette, a bead store in Duluth, Minnesota. She started out as a bead knitter, became hooked on beads, and has been working with this medium for the past 12 years.

Lynn B. Krucke (Summerville, South Carolina) is a mixed media artist whose interests include paper arts, beads, fiber, fabric, and polymer clay. In addition to her design work, Lynn teaches a variety of mixed-media classes.

Kelly Lightner (Asheville, North Carolina) has been beading for eight years, exploring many innovative aspects of the medium.

Dyan Peterson (Asheville, North Carolina) is a highly respected gourd artist. She is a member of the Southern Highland Craft Guild, founder of the Western North Carolina Gourd Society, and a teacher of gourd craft and basketmaking.

Susan Rind (Vancouver, BC, Canada) is the designer for Dustin Designs. She takes her inspiration from nature to create her chic home decor and fashion accessories line. She shows her work twice a year at the Pacific Designer Collection in New York City, and her work is retailed in gift galleries and exclusive clothing stores throughout the United States and Canada.

Virginia Saunders (Barnardsville, North Carolina) is an award-winning gourd artist from Barnardsville, North Carolina. She teaches gourd crafting and is a member of both the American and North Carolina Gourd Societies.

Debi Schmitz (LeMars, Iowa) has been designing from her home for over 10 years, specializing in designs for felt and fabric as well as dolls.

Brenda L. Spitzer (Wheaton, Illinois) is a certified craft designer in the Society of Craft Designers. She has been designing and teaching in the craft industry for 20 years.

Terry Taylor (Asheville, North Carolina) is a mixed media artist whose work has been shown in numerous exhibitions. He is an full-time employee of Lark Books.

Charli Traylor (Asheville, North Carolina) was introduced to beading as a child, but has been actively beading and bead weaving for the past five years. She teaches beading in the Southeast.

Nancy Worrell (Chapel Hill, North Carolina) is a free-lance author/designer who combines a variety of techniques and mediums to create unique paper, needlework, and fiberart designs. She is also the author of two books: *Paper Plus: Unique Projects Using Handmade Paper* and *Beautiful Wedding Crafts*.

INDEX